Understanding Home Construction

Perry Ennis

Southeastern Publishing Company

Dedication

To my parents, Dorothy and Jerry Ennis, and my mother and father-in-law, Naomi and Johnnie Edwards, who have taught me that love is the foundation that can make any house a home; and to my loving wife of 15 years, Debbie, who is my inspiration; and to the two precious children entrusted to us by God, Amanda and Joshua; and especially to you, the reader, who pursues the American dream of building and owning your own home, this book is dedicated.

Disclaimer

This publication is designed to provide accurate authoritative information in regard to the subject matter covered. It is sold with the understanding that the publisher is not engaged in rendering legal, accounting, or other professional service. If legal advice or other expert assistance is required the services of a competent professional should be sought.

Acknowledgments

I appreciate the professional work performed by the following people who have helped to make the publishing of this book possible: Sally Hamilton of Designer Type for typesetting; Barbara Manning, editing; Mark Elmore, cover artwork; Steven Baxter, illustrations; and Jean Utley, consultation.

Contents

Introduction 1

Section One: Preparing to Build 5
Chapter 1 . . . .Buying Your Lot 7
Chapter 2 . . . .Design and House Plans 11
Chapter 3 . . . .Making a Construction Cost Budget 33
Chapter 4 . . . .Your Construction Loan 41
Chapter 5 . . . .Loan Closings 55
Chapter 6 . . . .Scheduling, Permits and Inspections 61

Section Two: Construction Work, Description and Terminology 71
Chapter 7 . . . .Site Preparation 73
Chapter 8 . . . .Footings 75
Chapter 9 . . . .Foundations 77
Chapter 10 . . .Framing 81
Chapter 11 . . .Mechanical Systems 91
Chapter 12 . . .Plumbing 93
Chapter 13 . . .Heating and Air Conditioning 97
Chapter 14 . . .Electrical 103
Chapter 15 . . .Insulation 109
Chapter 16 . . .Interior Wall Finishing 115
Chapter 17 . . .Finished Flooring 119
Chapter 18 . . .Interior Doors and Trim Moldings 123
Chapter 19 . . .Cabinetry and Counter Tops 127
Chapter 20 . . .Mantles and Staircases .131

Section Three: Sweat Equity—How You Can Do It Yourself . .135
Chapter 21 . . .Hardwood Floor Finishing 137
Chapter 22 . . .Staining Cabinetry and Trim Moldings 141
Chapter 23 . . .Interior Painting 145
Chapter 24 . . .Wallpaper Hanging 147
Chapter 25 . . .Landscaping 149

Conclusion 155

Glossary 157

Index 167

Preface

Thank you for buying this book of information. I feel that you will find it to be concise and very helpful in understanding the process of residential contract building. You too can be successful at contracting the building of your own house just as I have been. I have written this book from my personal building and contracting experience. I am not a licensed contractor, nor have I done that type of work for a living. I chose to pursue the contract building of the home of our dreams for many reasons.

The most significant reason that I chose to contract the building of the home of our dreams was to save a large sum of money. We would not have been able to build our home when we did, or possibly ever, if we had not trimmed a lot off of the construction costs. I also wanted to be personally involved with each phase of the project to ensure quality workmanship.

It is very obvious that the cost of housing, whether new or old, has increased tremendously since the late seventies. During that time, rising interest rates slowed new house construction to a snail's pace. Mortgage interest hung in the mid-teens during the early eighties, and it caused unprecedented inflation in the building industry. Real estate, building materials and labor cost increases have risen to the point that an average income family is basically being driven out of the new house market.

There are many statistics that show the affordability of housing with comparisons from different years. The most discouraging figures are those that reflect the decrease of buying power that the average income family has to afford even a minimum-sized house. The salaries of average income, middle class working people have increased gradually over the years, but not nearly enough to keep up with the great increases of practically everything consumers buy—especially houses.

I contracted the building of our house out of pure necessity. My wife and I and two children were living in an 1100 square foot farmhouse that is about 100 years old. We were grateful to live there because the rent was very reasonable, allowing us to save money each month. As our children grew, the house became smaller and smaller. We knew we needed more space, but didn't want to go out and buy a larger house that wasn't really what we wanted. So for five years we lived in the small farmhouse, heating with a wood stove to save fuel costs, saving money each month and planning our dream house.

I believe that there is a natural desire in most people, a nesting instinct, to dream of and pursue having their very own dwelling. All through history, people of average or less than average incomes have had to sacrifice in order to afford a house of their own, especially a dream house.

When you're thinking about building a new house, the reality of the high cost of construction can be overwhelming. I know, because I have been there. If you are a young, married couple, eager to build a new house and save thousands, this book will help you to do that. If you and your family are rapidly outgrowing your present house and want to either add on more rooms or build a larger house, this book will help you to be able to afford to do so. If you are a retired person or couple who can't afford the high cost of construction to build the little cottage in the mountains or at the beach, this book will help you trim thousands off the bottom line and allow your dream cottage to become a reality.

Please read the introduction of this book before you proceed on with the text. The introduction will help you to understand the following material better and give you an example of how much money you can save on the construction of your house.

Perry Ennis

Perry Ennis
September, 1990
Greenville, North Carolina

Introduction

A house is a structure comprised of many different types of materials and is built by many different people who specialize in their field of work. A contractor is not required to know how to do all of the different types of work necessary to construct a house. It does help though to have a general knowledge of how the work is performed by each subcontractor and have an understanding of construction terminology. I have included a whole section of work description, plus a glossary and index, to help you to be more familiar with the many facets of the building process.

You don't have to know how to to build a set of custom-made kitchen cabinets in order to have them built. What is required if you are to be your own contractor in building a house is that you know what you want to build, be able to communicate with people, be assertive in planning and scheduling events for the project, be responsible for properly managing money and have a high degree of self confidence.

People of both sexes, from all races, and from many different occupations have successfully contracted the building of their own houses and saved substantial amounts of money. I have been a purchasing agent for the past nine years employed at a university. It was very challenging for me to maintain my job, help my school teacher wife with our two youngsters and build our dream house all at the same time. I am living proof, however, that it can be done.

The colored cut paper artwork of the house on the cover of this book is a perspective of the house my wife and I designed and for which I contracted the building. The house has four bedrooms, three baths, a kitchen, living room, dining room, utility room and pantry, totaling 2,370 square feet of heated space. There are 520 square feet of porch and 760 square feet of garage and workshop. On the back of the house are two decks. The lower deck is accessible through a door in the kitchen and is 12 x 16 feet. The upper deck is accessible through a French door in the master bedroom, and is 8 x 8 in dimensions. The house has many amenities, such as high performance windows, water source heat pump system, solid white oak kitchen cabinets with raised panel doors, lots of stained trim and doors, hardwood floors, custom staircase and mantle, and a large pantry. We were able to build our house for $37.10 per square foot for the heated space, porches and decks, and $11.92 per square foot for the unfinished garage. We saved approximately $7,500, or $3.16 per square foot, by doing the interior painting, staining, wallpaper hanging, hardwood floor finishing, and landscaping ourselves.

The total square footage cost of our house reflects the expense of labor and materials only. The cost of the lot, excavation, underground utilities, water line and well are all separate figures. The actual house construction figures are from the six months we were involved in building the house. We started on October 6, 1987 and finished April 12, 1988. The cost of labor and materials has increased some since then.

I received quotes from contractors to build our house in the summer of 1987. Most contractors figure the construction estimate by submitting a square foot cost for the heated area which will also include the building of the garages, porches, basements, decks and any amenities or extras that are specified in the plans. The going rate for basic house construction in our area is $45 to $47 per square foot. Since our house was designed with a large garage and workshop, double porches with concrete floors and several amenities and extras, the quotes averaged about $52 per square foot. We saved approximately $26,000 on our house due to my handling the contracting and our family and friends helping with the interior finishings.

Let's take a hypothetical situation and pretend that you are planning to build a 2000 square foot house with a 600 square foot garage, and like us, you have decided on some nice extras like hardwood floors. To allow for inflation since the time that I built, let's figure your heated area at $39 per square foot (which totals $78,000) and $17.50 per square foot for your finished garage (which totals $10,500) bringing your estimated total figure for the house to $88,500. The total construction quotes you get will vary greatly depending on where in the country you are building. Construction and housing costs in eastern North Carolina are lower than the average across the nation. Let's figure the contractor quotes that you have received for building this house at an average of $55 per square foot for the heating area only, which includes the total project turn key. So at $55 per square foot for 2000 square feet for the house and garage, this would total approximately $110,000. By contracting the project yourself, you should be able to save approximately $22,900 or 20% of the cost of what the contractor's figure would be. You can increase the percentage and the amount of money saved on the contracting of your house even more by doing some of the finishing work yourself. I have written a whole section in the back of this book called "Sweat Equity". This section will give you instructions on how to do a lot of the finishing work on a house which can help you save even more money.

Every $1,000 that you can save on your house building project is $1,000 that you don't have to borrow. By being able to shave many thousands of dollars off of what your mortgage would be if you paid full retail, your monthly payment will be much lower. You could also save enough by contracting the building of your house to finance your mortgage for a shorter term. There is a tremendous difference in the amount of interest paid between a 30-year mortgage and a 15-year mortgage for the same amount of money borrowed.

Wherever you are in your house building experience, whether you're trying to put together a plan to build your first house or a starter house, or if you're going for the ultimate dream house, you can save at least 20% of a contracted price of building your house by contracting the building of it yourself. An individual need not have a contractor's license in order to build his or her own house on his or her own property. The license is required if an individual is building a house for another person. A license may also be required by a lending institution if a person is applying for a construction loan in order to build his or her house. I have covered this information and how to approach a bank for a loan for the construction of your house in Chapter 4, entitled "Your Construction Loan."

I recommend that you study this book very carefully as you are working out your plans for the building of your house. I stress the importance of planning and scheduling events, as this is crucial to being successful with your project. Throughout the book are illustrations which will help you see and better understand certain phases of residential house construction. The boldfaced words are index words that are located on page 165. There are also samples of contracts, permits, blueprints, and other information that will help you to become more familiar with the total process of residential contract building.

I hope that this book will help you save as much of a percentage on your project as we were able to save on ours. If you follow its directions, your home building dreams can become a reality. My very best wishes to you in your building endeavor and I hope that once your project is completed and you have moved into your new home, you will enjoy it as much as my family and I enjoy our new home. You can do it. Go for it!

SECTION ONE

Preparing to Build

This is the most important section of this book because of the key information it contains relating to contracting. These chapters give you the instructions needed for the preparation and initiation of contracting the building of a house. It is absolutely imperative that all the many facets of your building project be thought through thoroughly before the construction begins. I encourage you to study your project in detail, just as you would study the material of a course for the final exam. Allow plenty of time to prepare your cost budget. Become familiar with the order in which the subcontractors come to perform their work on your project. Study Section Two so you will know what is involved with each subcontractor's work and construction terminology.

Please review this material several times while you are in the early planning stages of your project. It's very important that you fully understand all that is involved in the contracting of building a house, before you commit to doing it.

The more time you put into planning your project, the fewer mistakes will be made. Be assertive. Make as many decisions as possible before the construction work begins. Get into your project, but pace yourself. "Rome was not built in a day."

Chapter 1

Buying Your Lot

If you haven't bought a lot yet, there are some important things to consider. What are the aesthetics of where you want to live? Is the neighborhood and the location of it where you want to be? If you have selected a lot in a subdivision, will the house you want to build be acceptable there? Nearly all subdivisions have **restrictive covenants** which prevent people from having things such as livestock on their lot and will also indicate the minimum and maximum size that a house can be in that particular subdivision. You can't build a 2,000 square foot house in a subdivision that has a minimum square footage allowance for the house of 2800 feet.

If the lot has a slope, do you want to include a basement in your house plan? Does the lot have good drainage? The best way to find out is to observe the lot after a downpour. If it is not draining well, will it be corrected by the owner or can negotiating on the price of the lot be pursued? Does the lot offer city sewer, water, gas, trash collection, etc.? Be sure that you are getting your money's worth in the lot you choose. Check the sales price of lots nearby to see if they are compatible. Be careful in dealing with realtors. You can generally save three to six percent by dealing directly with the landowner who is subdividing his or her property into lots.

Always make a counter offer to a landowner. Sometimes they will reduce the asking sale price by ten percent or more. If you are not familiar with the area that you are considering, the services of a realtor or broker can be very helpful to you. Real estate agents are paid their commissions by the landowner and their loyalty is to that person. They earn their money by promoting the sale of the property. When pursuing the purchase of a lot through a real estate agent, let the agent work for the commission by providing you with all the needed information to help you make a decision on a lot. I have included, on the following page, some guidelines to assist you as you discuss a lot with a real estate agent and to help if you aren't working with one.

A. Land use **restriction** around the lot or zoning could mean that one side of a lot may be zoned residential and another side zoned commercial, which could have a negative impact at a later date.

B. If the lot is in the city limits, what does the city offer and how much does it cost?

C. Are there any types of easements on the property, such as city utilities underground easement?

D. If the lot is in a county rural area, has the lot passed the Health Department's test for a **septic tank system**? If it has, what is the going rate for a septic system and also for a well if needed?

E. Has the lot had a soil compaction test? It is important to have this test to insure that soil won't settle after a footing is poured and a house is built on it.

F. Is the lot in the path of known future government projects such as airports or interstate highways?

Many people are buying lots in suburbs and rural areas. Often in these areas there are no corporate sewer and water systems. Make sure you meet with a person from the Health Department to check out the lot you are interested in buying. The lot should drain well and pass all the septic drain fill requirements and the test borings for acceptable compaction. If the lot passes the soil and drainage percolation test and compaction test, and if you are still interested in buying it, a person from the Health Department will help you place your house around where he or she has determined where the **septic system** should be. As a general rule, it is better to place this system in the back yard. The side of your house the system is on will be approximately 100 feet from the property line.

If there is no water system nearby to tap into, you will have to have a **well** drilled. The distance requirements from a septic tank system to a well vary from state to state. In Pitt County, North Carolina, a well is required to be at least 50 feet from a septic tank or septic drain line in the system. The depth of the well will vary depending on how deep or large the water level is. If you have to have a well drilled, I recommend a four inch PVC pipe packed in gravel with a submersible water pump.

Before you sign a sales contract make sure it reflects as much information as possible about the lot you plan to purchase. Don't rush your decision to buy a lot. Walk over the property and review all the aspects of it several times until you feel comfortable with the purchase. One thing that you absolutely must do before you purchase any lot is to hire a real estate **attorney** to do a **title search** to make sure the property is free and clear of any encumbrances. This procedure should be performed by a real estate attorney only and should cost approximately $300, unless the title search is unusually involved.

The real estate **attorney** will research the ownership of the property back at least 40 years to check for defects in the title. If the attorney finds the property to be free and clear he or she should issue an opinion of title or a certificate of title verifying the results of his search. This verification from the attorney is required at a loan closing. It is a good idea to check around and hire a good real estate attorney at the beginning of your project. Not only will an attorney be needed at the beginning of the project, but also at the end for the loan closing. I have included information on loan closings in Chapter 5..

Another important person to establish an early rapport with is a reputable **surveyor**. If he is assisting you and the landowner by surveying a parcel of land which will be your lot, negotiate with him on a price for doing all of your survey work. You will need to have two more surveys performed during the course of your project, so he should take that into consideration and lower the total price for the surveys.

You should have your lot paid for and have a clear deed or title before you go to the bank for your construction loan. The bank will gladly use your lot for the down payment on your construction loan. This will also help you with your final mortgage in that your lot should represent at least 10% of your total **appraisal** value and therefore enable you to be in a 90% or less loan-to-value category.

Lots come in all sizes, shapes and types. Some people enjoy gardening and yard work so they purchase lots that have few or no trees on the lot. Others prefer no yard maintenance so they buy a wooded lot and have a few trees removed where the house site will be. Once the house is completed, they leave the yard in a natural state with basically no maintenance. This is great if it is what you want. Think and plan your project thoroughly to make sure your lot will offer what you really want.

It is very thrilling and exciting to be satisfied with the lot on which your house will ultimately stand.

Chapter 2

Design and House Plans

Debbie and I worked on our house plans and design for a year before we felt comfortable with them. We designed our entire house ourselves. I had ordered several house plan books. You know, the kind with 100 different floor plans and styles. These type books are good if you can find the style you want in a set of plans that work for you. We couldn't find what we wanted because we didn't really know what we wanted. After looking at several hundred different plans, we came to the conclusion that the only way we were going to get what we wanted was to design our own plans. We liked the exterior look of the two-story American traditional farm house with lap siding and large porches, so we started working up some perimeter dimensions from that style of exterior.

There are many styles to choose from. You may like the look of Williamsburg or something contemporary. I recommend that whatever you choose for an exterior look, you stay with that theme as you finish the interior of your house. The moldings, staircases, mantles and cabinetry should all compliment and blend with the exterior look of your house.

The right design and **floor plan** for your house is very important, especially if you have children or are planning to live in your new house a long time, or both. Our children were six and two when we moved into our house. We plan to raise our children in our house and hope one day to have our grandchildren come and visit in what will then be the old "homeplace."

To help you get a better feel for what you may want in a new house, ride around in subdivisions and look at newly constructed houses that are for sale. You can pick up good ideas on style, design, arrangement and decor this way. This is the best way to perceive what a 12 foot by 14 foot dining room with two piece chair rail, two piece crown with dental molding looks like. It's hard to visualize a house inside and out while staring at an artist pad or a set of blueprints.

We designed our house's floor plan with three main points of consideration. Convenience of practical arrangement of rooms was the first.

Second was energy efficiency, and third was views to the outside of the house. Your **floor plan** should flow from room to room so that you enjoy each aspect of your home. If you are designing yourself, use a large artist pad and draw your plan on one-half inch to one foot scale. This will be large enough so you can mentally get into each room and arrange windows, doors and furniture. The more time you spend in working out the details of your floor plan, the more it will help you when you are building.

We chose to build a rectangular two-story house because it was less expensive to build. It has less **roof** area and less foundation and is more energy efficient than a one-story house, plus, we liked the basic look of the house. It is also less expensive to build a house with a simple gable roof style without a steep pitch. A 12-12 pitch costs considerably more to build than a 7-12 pitch. If you choose a two-story house to build, please consider in the design a full bath and a room downstairs that can be used as a bedroom. We included in our design and construction of the downstairs bathroom and bedroom, extra wide doors that will accommodate a wheelchair. We never know what we may be confronted with in the future.

I spent a lot of time researching the construction of an energy efficient house. Some of the most productive time I spent was at the utilities office, talking with a man in the Energy Resources Department. I expressed to him that I wanted to build the most energy efficient house possible, without having to spend too much extra money.

The utility corporations sponsor a program called **E-300.** They want to help you to conserve electricity, especially if you are building a new house. They will take your completed floor plans and do a calculated heat gain/heat loss report on the efficiency of your house. At the conclusion of the report, they will give your house plans a score. If your plans score 300 or more, then your future house meets the criteria for being energy efficient. The main factors involved in this scoring process are: the number of windows and doors, placement of these (how many are on the north side, etc.), the type of exterior doors and windows, the type of heating and cooling system you choose and the insulation package you use.

The man from the Energy Resources Department went over the plans with me many times. This is what we concluded would be the best for our particular house. Our house has 28 windows, 10 of which are facing south. With this much glass, we had to go with high performance windows. For the money, I don't believe there is a better window than Andersen®. They are vinyl clad on the outside and never require painting. We chose metal insulated exterior doors with magnetic seals, like the one on your refrigerator door.

We decided to use a water source heat pump for our **heating and cooling system.** This system is presently the most efficient type on the market. Its initial cost is more than the same tonnage size in an air source heat pump, because of having to have a **well** for the water supply. We have a 2-ton unit upstairs and a 2-ton unit downstairs. With both units running in the heat mode, the water usage is approximately 12 gallons of water per minute. For cooling, it would be about 8 gallons per minute. Water from deep in the ground is constantly around 60 degrees. This type system extracts the heat or coolness from the water as it passes through. Small heat strips inside the units finish raising the temperature to the desired setting. The result is warmer air for less energy used, compared to the air system, which has very large kv heat strips that operate longer in order to heat frigid outside air. The water source system works the same way in the cooling mode, except it uses a refrigerant compressor to aid with the cooling.

If it is not feasible to go with the water source system, I would recommend a gas pack unit for heating and a highly efficient air condition unit for cooling. Your utilities personnel can be very helpful in advising you as to what size system your house should have, and the most up-to-date efficient types and brands of systems to meet your needs. They also have an **E-300** insulation package that you can submit to the insulation company you select for your house. This package specifies the types and thicknesses of insulation for the whole house, also where special caulking should be done in order to seal cracks.

By now you are probably saying "Wow, man, this thing is getting pretty involved!" I can remember when we were at this planning stage of the project. I was researching this and meeting with people about that, and trying to get feedback from my school teacher wife, and helping to care for two youngsters, and trying to find time to design and draw house plans while holding down a regular job. But I knew that one day it would be worth all our struggling. In the long run we would have built the house of our dreams, gotten the quality of construction we desired and saved a bunch of money. It all worked out as I believed it would. I have no regrets. You can do it too!

When you have worked on your plans and worked on your plans and worked on your plans until you want to rip them up into pieces, be patient. Grab hold of yourself and work on them a little more. Every little change you make with a pencil and eraser could mean thousands of dollars saved by making the change on paper rather than during the construction process. Subcontractors like tearing out and redoing new construction because they get to charge you extra, and some really sock it to you for after-the-fact changes.

Open up your mind and use your finger to walk through the doors. Look at where the windows are and visualize what it would be like to be in each room. Place receptacles, phone jacks, and heating and cooling vents where you think best. All this is important to work out in this planning stage before you have the plans drawn by a professional, or if you are modifying a set of purchased plans.

Once you are comfortable with the plans you have drawn, you are ready to have them drawn to quarter inch scale by a professional **draftsperson**. I don't recommend architects because they are very expensive for what they do. Check around. A lot of professional draftspeople draw **house plans** to diversify their incomes. They usually have an office in their home and will charge approximately $300 to $450 for six complete sets of plans. A complete set of plans must have a foundation drawing, an elevation drawing, a floor plan, and wall cross section. If you use an architect, you will receive an additional cabinet and vanity detail, a perspective and a complete materials specifications list. These extras are nice, but we couldn't see paying an extra $1,400 for them.

I have included at the end of this chapter a set of house plans to help you become more familiar with each drawing. Be sure that whoever makes your blueprints makes at least six complete sets for you. If you have ordered your house plans through the mail from a house plan company, make sure they have sent complete sets.

If you choose the draftsperson route, as we did, you will need to have a **materials list** take off. Draftspersons seldom include a material list with their plans. In most cities there are building supply houses that offer the service of estimating all of the materials that will be needed to build your house using your house plans as a guide. They will also, while estimating the materials and quantity, furnish a cost breakdown so you will have an estimate of the materials cost. As negotiations begin with subcontractors, you will find that the ones who do the plumbing, heating and cooling, electrical and insulation, will quote prices which include labor and all materials. Carpenters, whether framers or finishers, almost always charge by the square foot for their labor.

In going over the material list with the supply house estimator, you will have to be specific about many materials such as window brands, brick size and type, type of framing lumber, interior doors, cabinet and vanity materials, trim moldings, mantles, fireplace and chimney parts, shingle type and color, siding, brick veneer, masonite, wood or vinyl siding, and deck and porch materials. Try to make these decisions while the material list is being prepared. You will be way ahead when building actually starts. Once you have made the decision about which supply house to do business with, find one salesperson to handle your orders and help you to learn about building materials. There is a lot to know about building materials, and it is a good experience if you have a good teacher.

Plot Plan

On the following page is an example of a survey **plot plan** or plat. This plot plan is not ours. I borrowed it from a friend because I felt that a plot plan in a subdivision would be more relatable. This plat is usually drawn by the **surveyor** once you have made a definite decision on a house plan. It is important that this be drawn early in the project. Before any construction begins, review this with the city or county inspector to insure that your house is going to be acceptable on your lot. If you did your homework, as I suggested in Chapter 1, you will have learned of any easements, zoning set backs and right of ways from a survey map provided by the owner or real estate agent. If the foundation measurements of the house plan you've selected legally fit on the lot, you have a good match. If not, then you must decide on a larger lot or different house plan.

On pages 22 through 32 are the **house plans** my wife and I designed. It is 2,370 square feet heated, 760 square feet of garage and 520 square feet of porches, and 352 square feet of upper and lower decks. If you like this plan enough to build it for yourself, you will find an order form in the back of the book. Six complete sets of blueprints will be delivered to you for $225, much less than what it would cost you to have this plan drawn by a professional.

I would like to share ideas with you that we incorporated into the design and building of our house. These ideas should be helpful as you think through your project and visualize your finished house. Some of the features of our house are skylights on the south porch which allow extra light in through the large windows that are on either side of the fireplace. These skylights allow a lot of light into the living room during the winter and give the porch a nice touch.

We had gas logs with a blower installed in the fireplace which provide an excellent backup source of heat. By designing a large foyer with an open staircase above, heat from the logs circulate thoroughly throughout the second floor. The logs are 40,000 BTUs. With the blower operating, this system will heat the entire house, even on the coldest

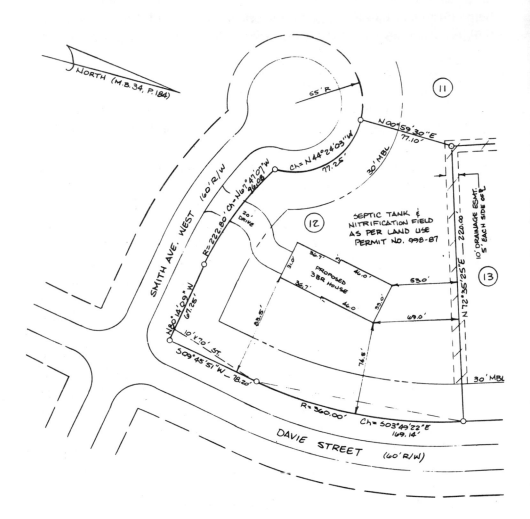

Plot Plan Diagram

nights.

The nooks in the kitchen and bedroom provide views of 180 degrees. We have made the nook in the master bedroom a small office with a love seat. I had the plumbers install water and drain lines in the back wall of the bedroom nook to have available for a future whirlpool.

We designed the kitchen cabinets to have a desk with drawers and glass cabinet doors. Every house needs a place where mail can be dropped for later reading.

We decided it would be a good idea to recess the steps from the garage into the hall. This design allows more room in the garage and breaks up what would have been a long hall.

The childrens' rooms are adequately large with built-in desks, shelves and cabinets. The closets have built-in shelves and a two-foot fluorescent light inside the closet above the door. This gives excellent light for the closets.

We designed the master bathroom to allow lots of room. A feature that we really like is the tiled shower which has two shower heads and two bench seats. If you and your spouse enjoy showering together, this shower design offers plenty of room and two places to sit while you shower or wash your feet.

Any house plan can be modified and rearranged. Doors and windows can be added or deleted and walls can be moved, as long as the foundation plan is also changed to insure the proper foundation support for load-bearing walls. Any changes that involve a change in the foundation should be performed by the draftsperson or architect.

I would like to offer some ideas that can enhance our floor plan, should you decide to build it and can afford these plan changes. It's currently a popular trend for two story houses with garages to have a **room** designed and built above the **garage**. We originally had this room in our design. After closely estimating our construction cost and weighing our space needs, we opted not to include the room. It was simply more than we could afford and we decided we could live without a playroom for the kids, which is what it would have been

If you truly want a room over the garage whether you choose our plan or any other, it can be accomplished with a few design changes. The floor joists will be nailed across either floor trusses, if you don't want support columns in the garage or girders which will have support columns under them. The other structure design change would be in the perimeter walls and roof pitch. A framing carpenter will be very helpful in showing you the best way to make this or any modifications of a house plan. On our plan, the access door to what would have been the room over the garage was located in the children's bathroom where the tub is now. When we decided not to build the room, we simply redesigned the bathroom and moved the tub around to the short wall where the door was.

Another design idea I will share with you concerning our house plan, is to build a screened-in porch in place of the lower deck. Above the screened-in porch a solarium would be nice. The second floor solarium would be an ideal place for a whirlpool or jacuzzi and possibly a media room. We hope to build these two rooms onto our house as soon as we can afford them.

These are some design ideas I wanted to share with you regarding our house plans that could be incorporated into any plan.

Perspective

See pages 22 and 23 for example of a 3-dimensional **perspective**. This type of drawing gives you a visual picture of what the best front view of the house should look like when it is finished.

Foundation Plan

Example of a **foundation** plan appears on pages 24 and 25. This plan is used by the footing contractor to lay out the batter boards for accurate measurement prior to digging the footing for the foundation walls and piers. The plan should show the size of the footings and the size and amount of reinforcement steel rods used.

This plan is also used by the mason subcontractor to build the foundation walls and piers, the chimney, if there is one, steps, and to install foundation vents. If the house plans include a basement, the foundation plan will have the location and dimensions of doors and windows.

First Floor Plan

On pages 26 and 27 is the first floor plan of our house. **Floor plans** are required to have the exterior wall dimensions, the location and dimensions of all windows and doors, fireplace, staircase, plumbing fixtures, cabinets and vanities. I recommend that if you are having the plans drawn locally, the draftsperson include all of the electrical receptacles, switches, overhead lights, phone jacks, location of the hot water heater, heating and cooling plant (even if it is an outside heat pump), closet rods and shelving, and a disappearing staircase to the attic if there is one. The more detailed the floor plan is, the more it will help you in are getting quotes.

The plan will be more self-explanatory.

Second Floor Plan

Pages 28 and 29 show the floor plan for the second floor of our house. All the essential information is included for this floor as is for the first floor plan.

Elevations

Pages 30 and 31 show the elevations of our house plan. The elevation drawings, show what the finished house will look like from all four sides.

Wall Cross Section

The **wall cross section** is on page 32. This illustration shows all of the materials used to build the perimeter walls of the house from the concrete footing to the shingles on the roof.

Specification Sheets

House plans generally will not have **specification sheets** unless they are drawn by an architect as they are quite expensive. They help the finish carpenters know more specifically what the dimensions, types of materials and hardware are for the kitchen cabinets, bathroom vanities and built-in bookcases. Spec sheets can also include molding schedules which will specify the size and type of trim moldings for each room. Expensive architectural drawings, can also include spec sheets for staircases, mantles and wet bars.

Materials Lists

I have included a part of the **materials list** from our plans on the following pages. A materials list is a take-off estimate of the type and quantity of the materials needed to build a house. This list varies in the amount of materials it includes. Generally it will include all estimated materials needed to dry the house in, outside veneer, sheetrock, shingles, and subfloor. Since insulation, electrical, plumbing, painting, wall paper hanging, and heating and air conditioning subcontractor quotes almost always include labor and materials, those materials won't be part of a regular materials list. You will need to break down and account for all of the cost related to your project by preparing a construction cost budget. The following chapter will help you to become familiar with how to do that.

You are moving along nicely once you get to this point. Most of the long hours of brain-straining and planning are behind you. When you get to this stage of pre-construction, you should have six complete sets of blueprint drawings, a materials list and a clear deed to your lot. But you are not ready to go to the bank yet. Before you go to the bank, you need a complete cost breakdown of all materials, labor and other related costs, to formulate a construction budget.

Materials List

Quantity	Unit	Description
56	PC	SL Pine Joist GM 2 2x10x14
37	PC	19/32 Rated Sheathing 40/20
4	EA	Bridging for 16 Ctr 50 PC Bdl 2x10
2	ROL	Poly 6 Mil Black 18 inx300'
300	CLF	SL Pine S4S or T&G 1x4 RL
2	PC	SL Pine Joist GM 2 2x12x10
3	PC	SL Pine Joist GM 2 2x12x14
1	HOM	Pkg 2 Wall Framing
480	EA	SPF Const Stud 2x4x93
100	EA	SPF Const or Std 2x4x12
70	EA	SPF Const or Std 2x4x16
34	PC	SPF Stud 2x6x93 (Pet)
90	EA	SPF Const or Std 2x4x10
1	HOM	Pkg 1 Floor System
2	PC	SL Pine Joist GM 2 2x10x8
2	PC	SL Pine Joist GM 2 2x10x10
3	PC	SL Pine Joist GM 2 2x10x12
1	PC	SL Pine Joist GM 2 2x10x14
3	PC	SL Pine Joist GM 2 2x10x16
30	PC	SL Pine Joist GM 2 2x10x14
14	PC	SL Pine Joist GM 2 2x10x10
30	PC	SL Pine Joist GM 2 2x10x16
36	PC	19/32 Rated Sheathing 40/20
4	EA	Bridging for 16 Ctr 50 PC BDL 2x10
308	EA	SPF Const Stud 2x4x93
35	PC	SPF Stud 2x6x93 (Pet)
6	EA	SPF No2 and BTR 2x6x12

62	PC	Black Tuff-R Sheath 1/2 IN 4x8
24	PC	15/32 Rated Sheeting 3 Ply 32/16
20	PC	Tuff-R Sheath 1/2IN 4x9
3	EA	SPF No2 and BTR 2x6x14
60	EA	SPF Const or Std 2x4x12
45	EA	SPF Const or Std 2x4x16
26	EA	SPF No2 and BTR 2x8x24
30	EA	SPF No2 and BTR 2x8x14
15	EA	SPF No2 and BTR 2x8x16
11	EA	SPF No2 and BTR 2x8x10
20	EA	SPF No2 and BTR 2x8x20
20	EA	SPF No2 and BTR 2x8x8
21	EA	SPF No2 and BTR 2x8x12
20	EA	SPF No2 and BTR 2x8x14
94	CLF	SPF/POND Pine 1/8 No2 S4S KD
6	PC	SL Pine Joist GM 2 2x10x16
2	PC	SL Pine Joist GM 2 2x10x14
2	PC	SL Pine Joist GM 2 2x10x12
50	EA	SPF No2 and BTR 2x8x8
56	EA	SPF No2 and BTR 2x6x12
84	EA	SPF No2 and BTR 2x6x22
14	EA	SPF No2 and BTR 2x6x8
25	EA	SPF Const or Std 2x4x12
21	EA	SPF Stud 2x4x96 (Pet)
117	PC	19/32 Rated Sheathing 40/20
10	ROL	Asphalt Fclt No 15 4 Square
129	BOL	OC Fiberglass Weathered Wood
2	EA	Treated Pine CCA 40 2x4x14 GM2
1	EA	Treated Pine CCA 40 2x10x8 GM2
1	EA	Treated Pine CCA 40 2x10x10 GM2
3	EA	Treated Pine CCA 40 2x10x12 GM2
4	EA	Treated Pine CCA 40 2x10x14 GM2
3	PC	SL Pine Joist GM 2 2x10x8
1	PC	SL Pine Joist GM 2 2x10x10
1	PC	SL Pine Joist GM 2 2x10x14
5	PC	SL Pine Joist GM 2 2x10x16
2	PC	SL Pine Joist GM 2 2x10x18
11	PC	Multi-purpose 2x2x12
25	PC	SL Pine Joist GM 2 2x10x8
8	PC	SL Pine Joist GM 2 2x10x10
32	PC	SL Pine Joist GM 2 2x10x12

Perspective Drawing

24

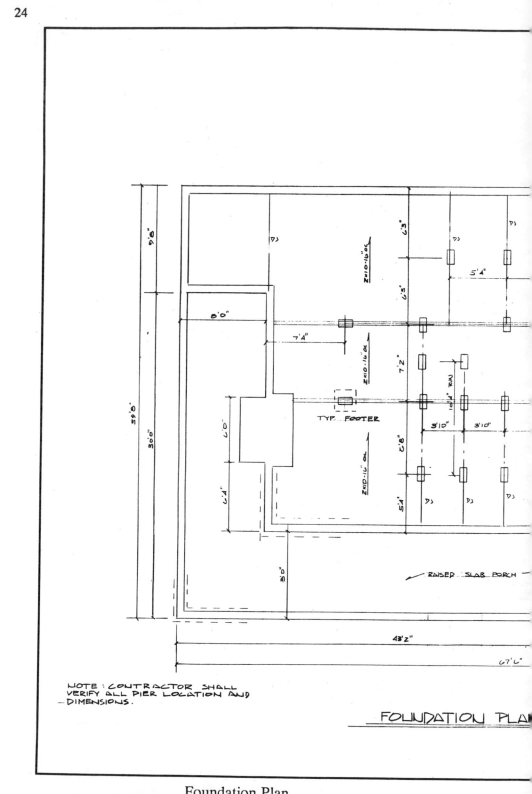

TYP. FOOTER

RAISED SLAB PORCH

NOTE: CONTRACTOR SHALL
VERIFY ALL PIER LOCATION AND
DIMENSIONS.

FOUNDATION PLAN

Foundation Plan

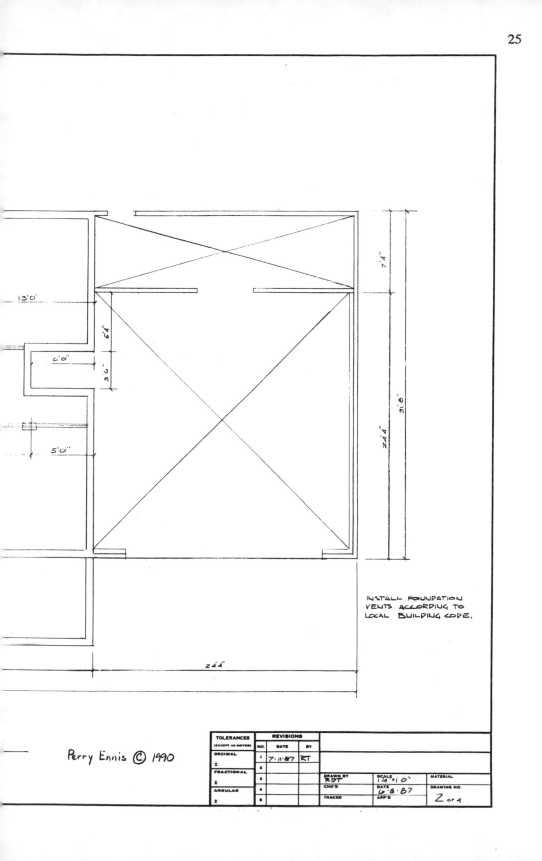

13'0"

6'0"

5'0"

7'4"

6'4"

3'6"

24'4"

31'6"

24'4"

INSTALL FOUNDATION
VENTS ACCORDING TO
LOCAL BUILDING CODE.

Perry Ennis © 1990

TOLERANCES	REVISIONS					
(EXCEPT AS NOTED)	NO.	DATE	BY			
DECIMAL	1	7-11-87	RT			
±	2					
FRACTIONAL	3			DRAWN BY RDT	SCALE 1/4"=1'0"	MATERIAL
±	4			CHK'D	DATE 6-8-87	DRAWING NO.
ANGULAR	5			TRACED	APP'D	2 of 4
±						

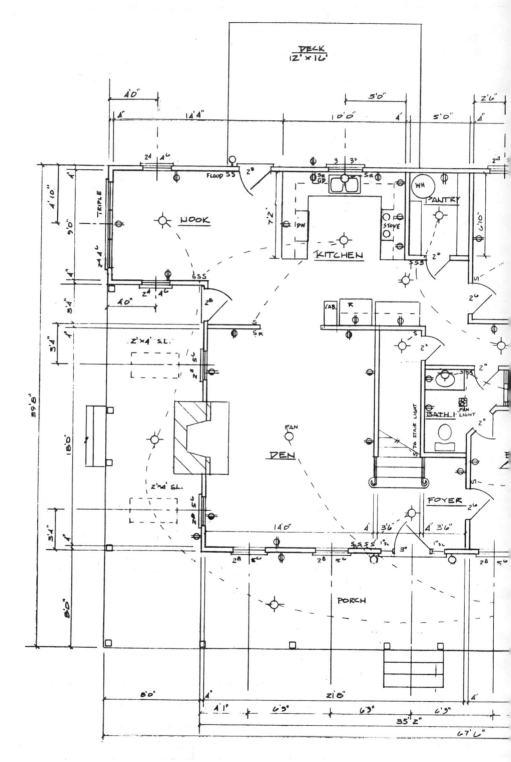

First Floor Plan

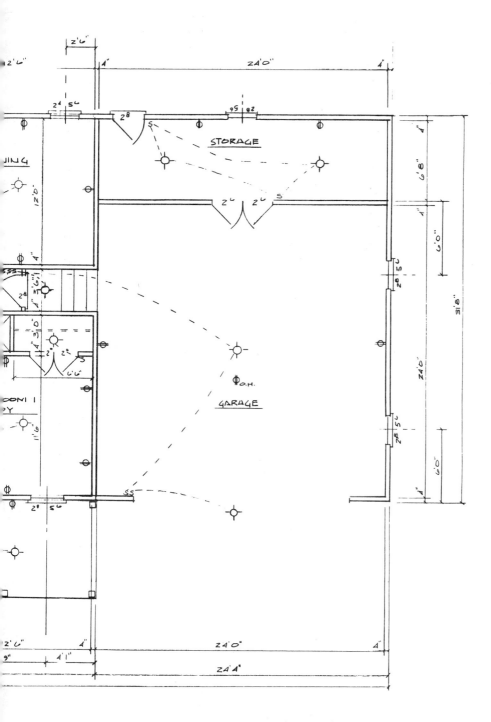

STORAGE

GARAGE

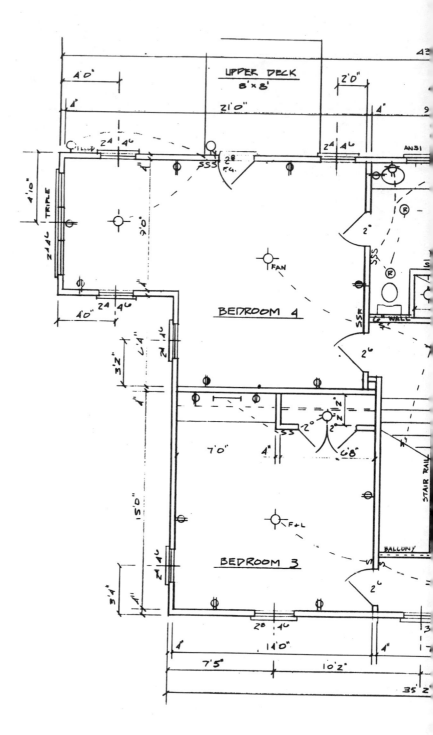

Second Floor Plan

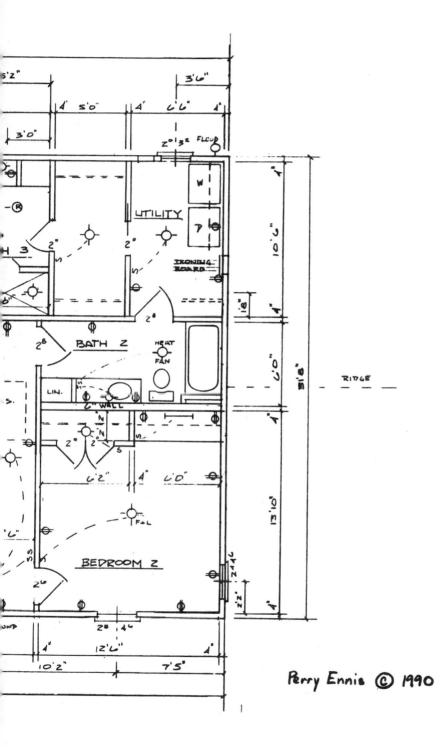

Perry Ennis © 1990

FROUT ELEVATIC
1/4" = 1'0"

RIGHT ELEVATION

REAR EL
1/8" = 1'0"

Elevations

‾ION   LEFT   ELEVATION

Perry Ennis © 1990

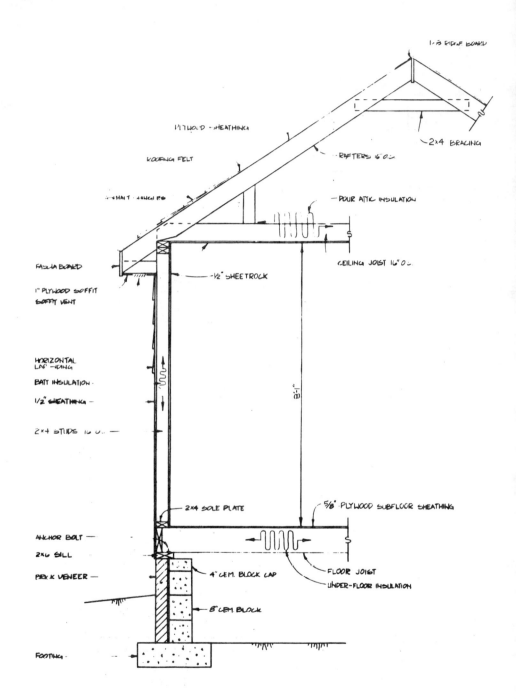

1×8 RIDGE BOARD

2×4 BRACING

PLYWOOD SHEATHING

ROOFING FELT

RAFTERS 16" O.C.

ASPHALT SHINGLES

POUR ATTIC INSULATION

FASCIA BOARD

CEILING JOIST 16" O.C.

1" PLYWOOD SOFFIT

1/2" SHEETROCK

SOFFIT VENT

HORIZONTAL
LAP SIDING

BATT INSULATION

1/2" SHEATHING

8'-1"

2×4 STUDS 16" O.C.

2×4 SOLE PLATE

5/8" PLYWOOD SUBFLOOR SHEATHING

ANCHOR BOLT

2×6 SILL

BRICK VENEER

4" CEM. BLOCK CAP

FLOOR JOIST

UNDER-FLOOR INSULATION

8" CEM. BLOCK

FOOTING

Wall Cross Section

Chapter 3

Making a Construction Cost Budget

Some who read this far may say to themselves, why did I buy this book? This house construction jazz is really involved. What is important to understand is, that if you have worked hard and have done a good job of working up your house plans and materials list, you will realize, while you are building, the small number of problems that will need to be resolved. The three most important principles in house construction contracting are: plan in detail, schedule all activity in advance and stay on budget.

You have already begun to make your **construction budget** by either receiving a materials list with your plans or asking the building supply salesperson to help you with a materials list and the cost of each item. Once you have the list, go to a copy machine, take a strip of paper and cover up the price columns. Make four or five copies of the list without prices. You can now begin to negotiate with other supply houses on the pricing of materials. Explain to them that you want their best contractor price and that if they are the overall lowest bidder, you will buy all of the materials from them. If you are satisfied with their materials and prices, apply for a credit account to be set up in your name. Once you have completed your bid results and have made your building supply house selection, you are ready to make your first entry figure for your budget. Add at least 5% to your total bid quote for unexpected materials and also possible price increases.

I remember that at this point I took one copy of the floor plan blueprint to a copy office that has a ledger-size reproducer and had about 12 copies made. This was very helpful in getting quotes from subcontractors. You want to get quotes from at least three different companies per type of work that needs to be done. As you get your floorplan copies back with the quotes, pass the copies on to the next sub that is bidding.

I have listed below, in A, B, C order, the **subcontractors** and other businesses that you will need to receive quotes from for your overall project budget. There is a brief description of the work and function of each subcontractor and business. There are also some suggestions for you to consider.

A. Lot Grading Contractor: He will take out trees, bring in dirt, place the driveway tile and grade your lot.

B. Health Department Inspector: If your lot is not in the city limits and requires a septic system, well, or both, then you should meet with an inspector from your local health department. He or she will tell you the price of a **septic system** permit. They will review the percolation test you requested before you bought the lot to determine what the septic system and general location of where your house-site should be.

C. **Surveyor:** As you are contacting surveyors for quotes, be sure to explain to them that you are contracting the building of your own house. Negotiate with them, explaining that you will need them to do a preconstruction survey, called a plat, and a final survey. They should give you a break on the price.

D. **Porta John Service:** In most places, it is required that this service be provided by a contractor for workers on construction projects.

E. Temporary **Phone:** I didn't have a temporary phone installed at our project site but, if I had it to go over again, I would. The small cost is insignificant when you consider the time it can save you driving to the project to make a decision you could have made on the phone. All calls should be local unless you are building long distance. If you decide to have a phone on your project site, designate the foreman or owner of the company that's working at your site each day to be responsible for the phone.

F. **Trash Container Company:** You will need to have a dumpster placed on your construction site and serviced at intervals. The alternatives are to hire a trash and debris removal company or if you have a pick-up truck, do it yourself. Its important to have construction debris removed as needed for safety reasons.

G. **Footings** Subcontractor: The footings subs accurately dig and pour the footings for your house. These subcontractors will need a copy of your foundation plans to figure their quotes. Their quotes should include: (1) batter board material needed; (2) rebar steel; and (3) concrete.

H. **Mason** Subcontractor: The masons will probably give you a separate quote for the foundation, steps, chimney, and brick veneer, if you select brick veneer.

I. **Framing** Subcontractor: It was my experience, that the most important subcontractor of our project was the framing subcontractor.

Once you have found a **framing** subcontractor that you feel comfortable with, go over your plans with him. He should be very helpful in assisting you with decisions on floor plan changes and ways to save money. Sometimes a slight change of the roof pitch can mean a savings of several hundred dollars. The framer will quote to you his price for drying in your house. Generally a framer will quote separately for siding, boxing of the exterior, porches, garages and decks. This is because they figure each process at a different price per square foot.

J. **Plumbing** Company: The plumbing company estimator will give you a quote for plumbing materials and labor. As you are discussing your house with different companies, you should make decisions on your tub, toilet, lavoratory and kitchen fixtures, such as style and color.

K. **Heating and Air Conditioning Company**: With the help of the Energy Services Department, you should have decided on the type and size of system you need for your house. In dealing with all of the subcontractors you select for your project, make sure that they are reputable.

L. **Electrical Company**: The electrical company estimator will give you a quote for all materials and labor just as the plumbing, heating and air conditioning companies will. It's a good idea to price electrical fixtures at this time so you will have a complete cost estimate for your budget ledger.

M. Insulation Company: Be sure to specify the **E-300** program if you have selected it.

N. **Sheetrock** Installation Subcontractor: The estimator for this company will give you a quote for hanging, finishing, and spraying ceilings. If you plan to have painted ceilings, be sure to specify that to him.

O. Finish Carpentry Subcontractor: Like the framing subcontractor, the finish carpentry sub will give you a quote for each area of finish carpentry work. The different types of work will include, finish flooring, cabinets, vanities, mantles, shelving, hanging interior doors, casing windows and doors, all moldings and installing staircases, if you house has one. Be as specific as you can when discussing your interior finish.

P. Cement Finishing Subcontractor: This sub will quote you for pouring and finishing the cement for your garage, driveway, sidewalks and porch floor. It's important to stress to him the need for expansion joints whenever necessary.

Q. Paint and Stain Subcontractor: Make decisions as soon as you can concerning whether to paint or stain the cabinetry and moldings in your house. Generally painters prefer that the contractor furnish all materials and will quote only on their labor.

R. **Wallpaper** Hanger: When you are asking for prices from these subs, ask them to figure in time for applying wall sizing. This will add a little to the quote, but will make removing the wallpaper easy if you ever wanted to change the wallpaper.

S. Carpet and Vinyl Company: The cost of quality carpet and vinyl varies a lot. Floor covering has become very diversified over the years, with so many brands, types and styles to choose from. Be sure to read thoroughly Chapter 17 entitled "Finished Flooring" for tips on selecting quality floor coverings before you begin soliciting quotes.

T. Appliance Company: Price appliances for the features you want. Make sure that you know the size of your appliances so that they will fit in the spaces that are designed in the cabinet layout. I recommend that you select the appliances you want for you kitchen before you meet with your cabinet maker, or before you order prefabricated cabinets.

U. Landscape Company: Whoever does your **landscaping** will put the finishing touch on the exterior look of your house. There's a lot to know about creating a beautiful yard. Study Chapter 25 to help you become familiar with landscaping. You may want to do it yourself. If you bid out the work to companies, you will find a lot of difference in prices. It's best to have a complete landscape layout of all that you want in your finished yard to give to each company to bid on. I recommend that you make copies of the perspective or front elevation of your house plans to use to work up your layout of shrubs and trees.

I found it very helpful while negotiating quotations with all of the **subcontractors,** to talk with them about the building time of our house. You can generally allow about two to three weeks from the time you apply for a construction loan until the time you have the actual funds to work with. This will help you have a general start-up date that you can discuss with the subcontractors.

I have included the pre-construction cost budget that I did for our house on pages 38 and 39 as an example of all materials, subcontactors' costs, permits and miscellaneous expenses. It is important to have the construction cost budget prepared so that the bankers you meet with will have a cost breakdown of where the construction loan money will be spent.

It's smart to add at least 5% to the total bottom line cost to allow for unexpected cost increase on materials, or minor changes that you may decide to make while you are in the building process.

Keep all of the bids or quotes that you receive from the subcontractors organized by trade. It's a good idea to start a small file. An empty copy paper box works good for this purpose.

Take your time reviewing the subcontractor's bids. Check out their work and ask questions to people that they have done work for. You want to make sure that you are hiring good, competent people to build your house. Be sure you have a signed **contract**, specifying the work they will perform for their cost bid, before they begin work. I have included a sample contract form on page 40. Be sure your attorney approves whatever form you use.

PRE-CONSTRUCTION START-UP COSTS
August, 1987

House Plans	$500.00
Grading, excavation	850.00
1" Water meter and temporary spigot hook-up	520.00
Temporary electrical service pole with receptacles	140.00
Title search by lawyer	350.00
Building permit	220.00
Builder risk insurance	307.00
Construction Loan Closing	1,225.00
Total	$4,112.00

($1.73 per square foot)

COST ESTIMATE FOR MATERIALS AND LABOR - HOUSE, PORCHES AND DECKS

Digging and pouring footing for foundation; labor	$750.00
Masonry labor for foundation piers, and curtain wall, fireplace, chimney	2,600.00
Pest control application	350.00
Concrete, bricks, blocks, lumber, roofing, doors, nails windows, stairs, sheetrock, plywood, flooring, hardware	33,000.00
Labor for framing, boxing and concrete pouring	6,300.00
Plumbing; all fixtures, pipe, hot water heater; labor	5,400.00
Roofing labor	550.00
Electrical; all wiring, panel box, breakers, labor and fixtures	4,200.00
Heating and air conditioning; two Rudd Hi-eff. water source units, duct and labor	5,800.00
Vinyl siding; all house, porch, ceiling; labor	5,400.00
Insulation; E-300 rating, total house	1,900.00
Sheetrock labor; hanging, finishing, spraying ceilings	1,950.00
Finish carpentry labor; cabinets, (kitchen, baths, children's rooms), hardwood floors, trimming all rooms with 1 pc. crown, 1 pc. chair, 1 pc. base and staircase	6,350.00
Paint and stain materials	690.00
Mirrors, towel racks, wallpaper	380.00
Vinyl flooring, material and labor	530.00
Carpet, padding, installation	3,700.00
Septic tank and system	1,950.00

Landscaping, grading, seeds, shrubs, trees	500.00
Well, with submersible pump	1,500.00
Total	83,800.00
	($35.36 per square foot)

GARAGE

Concrete, bricks, lumber, roofing, doors, windows	$6,800.00
Labor for framing, boxing and concrete pouring	1,180.00
Roofing labor	120.00
Vinyl siding labor and materials	960.00
Total	9,060.00
	($11.92 per square foot)
Total Cost of Project	$96,972.00
	($40.92 per square foot)

Proposal

PROPOSAL SUBMITTED TO	PHONE	DATE
STREET	JOB NAME	
CITY, STATE AND ZIP CODE	JOB LOCATION	
ARCHITECT	DATE OF PLANS	JOB PHONE

We hereby submit specifications and estimates for:

We Propose hereby to furnish material and labor — complete in accordance with above specifications, for the sum of:

_____ dollars ($ _____).

Payment to be made as follows:

All material is guaranteed to be as specified. All work to be completed in a workmanlike manner according to standard practices. Any alteration or deviation from above specifications involving extra costs will be executed only upon written orders, and will become an extra charge over and above the estimate. All agreements contingent upon strikes, accidents or delays beyond our control. Owner to carry fire, tornado and other necessary insurance. Our workers are fully covered by Workmen's Compensation Insurance.

Authorized
Signature _____

Note: This proposal may be
withdrawn by us if not accepted within _____ days.

Acceptance of Proposal — The above prices, specifications and conditions are satisfactory and are hereby accepted. You are authorized to do the work as specified. Payment will be made as outlined above.

Signature _____

Date of Acceptance: _____

Signature _____

Sample Contract Form

Chapter 4

Your Construction Loan

Ah yes, things are getting interesting at this point. You are about to make some of the biggest monetary decisions and commitments of your life. Before you start talking to bankers, run down a little checklist. You've got a <u>clear deed</u> to your lot that is paid for. You've got six full sets of construction <u>blue prints</u> of the house that you are confident you want to build and a detailed line item <u>cost budget</u> that reflects all the cost of building your house. You have gained <u>valuable knowledge</u> from spending time talking with the building supply salesperson, all of the sub-contractors that you've gotten quotes from, the surveyor, your attorney, and the people from the building inspector's office. Now that you have prepared yourself, you are ready to meet the person that will loan you the money to make your dream become a reality. It will be up to you, once you have selected a banker, to prove to that person that you know what you are doing, that you have the resources to build your house and that you are committed to seeing the project through.

Continue with the process of getting quotes from the **bankers** just as you did with the subcontractors. They all have different rates, closing costs, policies and stipulations. The banker with the lowest interest rate may not be the best one to work with. Just as you have felt out the sub-contractors, do the same with the bankers. You definitely want to do business with a banker who is personable, flexible, understanding and who truly wants to help you build your house. Remember, bankers are in the business of making money by lending money. They want to loan money to people with good credit, that they can trust. They are going to want to know about your financial history, your current indebtedness, and your salary to determine if you are a good risk. It's a good idea to talk to these various bankers that you are feeling out about **mortgages**, so that you can begin learning what your options are. You can save some money at closings by financing your mortgage through the same bank that is supplying your construction loan. The banking industry can be complex to understand, so you have to ask a lot of questions. Don't be intimidated or bashful.

It is very important to find out from the bank you choose to do business with, when they will do the closing for the **construction loan**. Some require it at the beginning of the loan, others at its completion. The closing will involve your **attorney**, who makes all the documents legal and binding. Closing costs can include a 1% origination fee, title search fee, the lawyer's fee, and several other related costs that need to be thoroughly checked out. Ask a lot of questions up front so that you know how much cost you are in for at the closing. A construction **loan closing** can cost from $500 to as much as $5,000 or $6,000, depending upon the **bank** and how much they want to make on a term loan. Keep smiling, it will all be worth it one day.

In the State of North Carolina, an individual can legally build one house per year on his or her own lot, without having to have a contractor's license if they aren't financing any money to build. The laws regarding this will vary from state to state. Banks have rules and regulations that are used to qualify or disqualify a loan. Most banks require an individual applying for a construction loan to be a licensed contractor. Some banks are more flexible. If you find a banker that you feel good about, whose bank has a policy of requiring a submitted contract from a licensed contractor to accompany the construction loan, this is what you can do. Talk to your relatives and friends. In the network of people you know, somebody has a friend or associate that is a licensed contractor who is building houses. This is what I had to do in order to get my construction loan from the bank that I chose to do business with.

I have a friend who knew a licensed contractor. I called the contractor and introduced myself, told him of my friend's referral, and briefly conveyed my plans and situation with the bank. He was interested in helping me and we made an appointment to meet at his home. I went to his home and showed him my house plans and cost budget. He was impressed with all of the leg work and time I had put into the budget preparing for the loan request. He said he would help me get the construction loan and give advice as I needed it during the project. I offered him a fee for his services and he accepted and became my **contractor associate**. His fee was very reasonable and he signed the contracts at the bank with me in order to qualify the construction loan. I found this man to be a very kind and understanding person who is now a close friend.

This type of arrangement between you and a licensed contractor is given a variety of names, and can have different degrees of involvement by the contractor. My banker called it a "wrap- around" contract. The licensed contractor who signed with me at the bank did not have any involvement in the actual building process, so his fee was very small.

If you are not comfortable with the idea of taking full responsibility for your building project, negotiate with your contractor to establish how much you want him or her involved. The more the contractor is involved, the higher the contractor's fee will be.

You may want your **contractor associate** to sign with you, help you to locate reputable subcontractors and simply check in on your project a week or so before inspectors to make sure your project is going well and on schedule. This arrangement should justify a modest fee because the contractor is not performing the coordinating, scheduling, legwork and money managing that is associated when a contractor assumes a turn-key project.

The point I hope to convey here is to find someone who is licensed and reputable that you can work with who can give you some initial guidance if you feel you need it.

You can imagine that as I left my contractor associate's house the night he agreed to sign with me, I was beaming from ear to ear. As I was driving back to my home, I let out a big hallelujah! A great burden had been lifted from my shoulders. I knew that now I would be able to qualify the construction loan I needed to build our house.

This is the type of tenacity you must have when attempting a project of this magnitude. Be persistent; don't give up. If you truly want to build your dream house and save a lot of money, you will find a way to do it, no matter how many obstacles you encounter.

Once you have selected the banker and banking institution that you want to do business with, and the bank has agreed to back your loan, it would be a good time to open a separate checking account for your construction transactions. You definitely want to keep all of your construction related transactions separate from your personal account.

Banks require that there be an **appraisal** of your house plans before the construction loan is approved. This appraisal is important to you and the bank. It ensures the bank that they are not loaning more money than what the property would actually be worth on the market once completed. Banks back their loans with collateral. The appraisal is done by a private, independent firm that will assess the value of what the completed house will be. Amenities are figured into their assessment process. Be sure to have a list of all the nice extras you are putting into your house that are not included in the house plans. The cost for the appraisal that was done on our house was $250. The cost for doing an appraisal will vary from location to location. Generally, the bank's policy is that they will select the appraisal company that they want to do the appraisal on the house plans. Your banker will call you when he has received the completed appraisal and discuss it with you during a meeting.

Now you are really getting down to business. The banker will schedule a meeting between you, and your spouse if you are married, and your **contractor associate**, if he is required to be there to sign the construction loan forms. My contractor associate submitted a signed contract from his company for the amount we were borrowing to build the house. My banker knew that I was actually going to be the builder of the house, but he needed a contract to comply with the policies of his **bank**. From that point on my contractor associate was not involved in any transaction or any of the building process. Once all the paperwork was finalized, we were all very happy and excited about the ground breaking.

Banks will generally establish a **construction loan** for a period of one year. You will probably not need that much time, but it's nice to know you have it if you do need it. You should be able to build your house from digging the footings to installing carpet in six months or less. We built ours in almost exactly six months and were building through the winter, which slowed our process some.

After your construction loan is processed and available, your banker will give you a percentage of completion sheet that qualifies the amount of money the bank will give you on each draw. I have included a blank copy of the actual sheet that we used on page 46. This will illustrate the breakdown of how the money was disbursed on the dates that the percentage of construction work was actually completed.

A **draw** is a portion of the total building funds. This is important. If you are building an average size house of around 2,000 square feet, you should have at least $5,000 of start-up money to carry you until you receive the first draw. I will give you an example of how this works. Let's say you have good weather and have made a lot of early progress on your house. The footings have been dug and poured, the foundations are in and the house has been framed. You are ready for your first draw, because you have used most of your start-up money to pay your subcontractors. They are usually small businesses and like to be paid weekly for their labor. All your materials have been charged at the building supply house, and it's been about a month since your first materials were charged. You call your banker to let him know that you are ready for your first draw. He may or may not be able to go to your house site for an inspection. You meet with him and go over the percentage of work completed that you have filled out on your completion sheet. These figures are examples because all bank forms are different. The lot grading is 2%; the water hookup is 1%; the footings and foundation totals 3%; the framing with windows and doors is 7%; and the roof is 4%. If you are borrowing $80,000, each percent would equal $800. For your first draw you have 17% completion, so your banker will cut you a check for $13,600. This money will enable you to pay what is due at the supply house and give you cash flow for your next group of subcontractors. It's very important to study your budget and anticipate the percentage of completions in order to make your draws work out right. **Banks** generally allow six draws for residential construction projects, which enables you to have one draw per month.

The bank will also require a form called a description of building materials that you will need to fill out. It's not complicated, but you may want to sit down fifteen minutes with your **contractor associate** to go over it. I have included a sample of the standard form used in North Carolina, issued by the bank, on the following pages.

The bank will also require you to have a **builder's risk insurance** policy.

Your progress is really moving along now. The anticipation of hearing saws running and seeing boards being nailed together is building inside of you. There is just one more important procedure and that is to work up a schedule. Study Chapter 6, Scheduling, Permits and Inspections, to learn more about your construction schedule. You are now beginning to understand why contractors charge 15 to 20 percent and more to build houses for people. There is a lot of planning and coordination in residential construction.

RESIDENTIAL CONSTRUCTION INSPECTION AND DISBURSEMENT REPORT

Borrower _____ Loan # _____

Lot _____ Block _____ S/D _____ St. Address _____

Appraised Value $ _____ _____ % = Construction Loan $ _____

Less Lot Loan $ _____ Balance to be Pro-rated in % Below $ _____

Lot Release Amount $ _____

ITEMS COMPLETED	%	1st	2nd	3rd	4th	5th	6th	7th	8th	9th
Clear lot - Rough grade	3									
Footings	1									
Foundation — Slab	4									
Floor Framing ( ) Sub-Floor ( )	5									
Walls: O/S Studs ( ) I/S Studs ( ) Wall sheating ( )	7									
Roof framing ( ) roof sheathing ( )	6									
Heating roughed in	2									
Plumbing roughed in	4									
Wiring roughed in	2									
Roofing shingles	2									
Outside doors and windows ( ) Insulation ( )	5									
Siding/Veneer	7									
Inside wall & ceiling: Rough ( ) Finished ( )	7									
Inside trim	4									
Inside doors	3									
Interior painting - primed	1									
Interior painting complete	2									
Exterior trim	2									
Exterior painting - primed	1									
Bath floors ( ) Wall tile ( ) Shower Stall ( )	3									
Furnace ( ) hot water heater ( )	4									
Plumbing fixtures	3									
Cabinets	3									
Appliances	2									
Concrete drive ( ) walks ( )	2									
Electrical fixtures set	1									
Septic tank ( ) sewer ( ) water ( )	2									
Floor finish ( )	1									
Gutter & downspouts	1									
Exterior painting - Complete	1									
Air conditioning	3									
Main floors - hardwood ( ) carpet ( )	4									
Finish grading ( ) clean up ( ) landscape ( ) screens ( )	2									
TOTALS	100									
INSPECTED BY (Initials)										
DATE INSPECTED										

NOTE: BEFORE DISBURSING — CHECK LEDGER BALANCE WITH BALANCE SHOWN BELOW. IS INTEREST CURRENT?

INSPECTION NUMBER	DATE OF INSPECTION	% COMPLETED This Advance	% COMPLETED To Date	AMOUNT ADVANCED	BALANCE OUTSTANDING	REMARKS
LOT LOAN						
1						
2						
3						
4						
5						
6						
7						
8						
9						

Lot _____ Block _____   Loan Fee $ _____   Survey Rec'd. _____

Loan # _____   Deduct From First Draw _____   Builders Risk $ _____

Invoiced Date First Draw _____   Policy No. _____

Date Paid _____   Item No. _____

Expires _____

_____

Percentage of Completion Sheet

DESCRIPTION OF MATERIALS

❏ Proposed Construction

❏ Under Construction

No. _____

(To be inserted by HUD, VA or FmHA)

Property Address _____ City _____ State _____

Mortgagor or Sponsor _____   _____
                              (Name)   *Address*

Contractor or Builder _____   _____
                              (Name)   *Address*

INSTRUCTIONS

1. For additional information on how this form is to be submitted, number of copies, etc., see the instructions applicable to the HUD Application for Mortgage Insurance, VA Request for Determination of Reasonable Value, or FmHA Property Information and Appraisal Report, as the case may be.

2. Describe all materials and equipment to be used, whether or not shown on the drawings, by marking an X in each appropriate check-box and entering the information called for each space. If space is inadequate, enter "See misc." and describe under item 27 or on an attached sheet. THE USE OF PAINT CONTAINING MORE THAN THE PERCENTAGE OF LEAD BY WEIGHT PERMITTED BY LAW IS PROHIBITED.

3. Work not specifically described or shown will not be considered unless required, then the minimum acceptable will be assumed. Work exceeding minimum requirements cannot be considered unless specifically described.

4. Include no alternates, "or equal" phrases, or contradictory items. (Consideration of a request for acceptance of substitute materials or equipment is not thereby precluded.)

5. Include signatures required at the end of this form.

6. The construction shall be completed in compliance with the related drawings and specifications, as amended during processing. The specifications include this Description of Materials and the applicable Minimum Property Standards.

---

1. **EXCAVATION:**
   Bearing soil, type _____

2. **FOUNDATIONS:**
   Footings: concrete mix _____ ; strength psi _____ Reinforcing _____
   Foundation wall: material _____ Reinforcing _____
   Interior foundation wall: material _____ Party foundation wall _____
   Columns: material and sizes _____ Piers: material and reinforcing _____
   Girders: material and sizes _____ Sills: material _____
   Basement entrance areaway _____ Window areaways _____
   Waterproofing _____ Footing drains _____
   Termite protection _____
   Basementless space: ground cover _____ ; insulation _____ ; foundation vents _____
   Special foundations _____
   Additional information: _____

3. **CHIMNEYS:**
   Material _____ Prefabricated (make and size) _____
   Flue lining: material _____ Heater flue size _____ Fireplace flue size _____
   Vents (material and size): gas or oil heater _____ ; water heater _____
   Additional information: _____

4. **FIREPLACES:**
   Type: ❏ solid fuel; ❏ gas-burning; ❏ circulator (make and size) _____ Ash dump and clean-out _____
   Fireplace: facing _____ ; lining _____ ; hearth _____ ; mantel _____
   Additional information: _____

5. EXTERIOR WALLS:
Wood frame: wood grade, and species_____ ☐ Corner bracing. Building paper or felt _____
Sheathing _____; thickness _____; width _____; ☐solid; ☐ spaced ____" o.c.; ☐ diagonal; _____
Siding_____; grade _____; type _____; size _____; exposure _____"; fastening_____
Shingles_____; grade _____; type _____; size _____; exposure _____"; fastening_____
Stucco _____; thickness _____"; Lath _____; weight _____lb.
Masonry veneer_____ Sills _____ Lintels _____ Base flashing _____
Masonry: ☐ solid ☐ faced ☐ stuccoed; total wall thickness __"; facing thickness ____"; bonding _____
Door sills _____ Window sills _____ Lintels _____ Base flashing _____
Interior surfaces: dampproofing, _____coats of _____; furring _____
Additional information: _____
Exterior painting: material _____; number of coats _____
Gable wall construction: ☐ same as main walls; ☐ other construction _____

6. FLOOR FRAMING:
Joists: wood, grade, and species _____; other _____; bridging _____; anchors _____
Concrete slab: ☐ basement floor; ☐ first floor; ☐ ground supported; ☐ self-supporting; mix ____; thickness ____ ";
reinforcing _____; insulation _____; membrane _____
Fill under slab: material _____; thickness _____".
Additional information: _____

7. SUBFLOORING: *(Describe underflooring for special floors under item 21.)*
Material: grade and species _____; size _____; type _____
Laid: ☐ first floor; ☐ second floor; ☐ attic ____ sq. ft.; ☐ diagonal; ☐ right angles.
Additional information: _____

8. FINISH FLOORING: *(Wood only. Describe other finish flooring under item 21.)*

LOCATION	ROOMS	GRADE	SPECIES	THICKNESS	WIDTH	BLDG. PAPER	FINISH
First floor							
Second floor							
Attic floor _____ sq. ft.							

Additional information: _____

9. PARTITION FRAMING:
Studs: wood, grade, and species _____size and spacing _____Other _____
Additional information: _____

10. CEILING FRAMING:
Joists: wood, grade, and species _____Other _____Bridging _____
Additional information: _____

11. ROOF FRAMING:
Rafters: wood, grade, and species _____Roof trusses (see detail): grade and species _____
Additional information: _____

12. ROOFING:
Sheathing: wood, grade, and species _____; ☐ solid; ☐ spaces ___" o.c.
Roofing _____; grade _____; size _____; type _____
Underlay _____; weight or thickness ___; size _____; fastening _____
Built-up roofing _____; number of plies _____; surfacing material _____
Flashing: material _____; gage or weight_____; ☐ gravel stops; ☐ snow guards
Additional Information: _____

13. GUTTERS AND DOWNSPOUTS:
Gutters: material _____; gage or weight_____; size _____; shape_____
Downspouts: material _____; gage or weight___; size _____; shape _____; number __
Downspouts connected to: ☐ Storm sewer; ☐ sanitary sewer; ☐ dry-well. ☐Splash blocks: material and size _____
Additional information: _____

14. LATH AND PLASTER
Lath ❑ walls, ❑ ceilings: material_____; weight or thickness ___ Plaster: coats _____ ; finish
Dry-wall ❑ walls, ❑ ceilings: materials _____; thickness _____; finish _____ ;
Joint treatment_____

15. DECORATING: *(Paint, wallpaper, etc.)*
ROOMS   WALL FINISH MATERIAL AND APPLICATION   CEILING FINISH MATERIAL AND APPLICATION
Kitchen_____
Bath _____
Other _____
_____
Additional information:_____

16. INTERIOR DOORS AND TRIM:
Doors: type _____; material _____; thickness _____
Door trim: type_____; material _____ Base: type _____; material _____; size _____
Finish: doors _____; trim _____
Other trim (item, type and location)_____
Additional information:_____

17. WINDOWS:
Windows: type_____; make _____; material _____; sash thickness_____
Glass: grade _____; ❑ sash weight; ❑ balances, type _____; head flashing _____
Trim: type _____; material _____ Paint _____; number coats _____
Weatherstripping: type _____; material _____ Storm sash, number _____
Screens: ❑ full; ❑ half; type _____; number _____; screen cloth material _____
Basement windows: type_____; material _____; screens, number _____; Storm sash, number __
Special windows _____
Additional information:_____

18. ENTRANCES AND EXTERIOR DETAIL:
Main entrance door: material_____; width _____; thickness _____". Frame: material _____; thickness "
Other entrance doors: material _____; width _____; thickness _____". Frame: material _____; thickness "
Head flashing_____Weatherstripping: type __; saddles _____
Screen doors: thickness __"; number__; screen cloth material __ Storm doors: thickness _____"; number _____
Combination storm and screen doors: thickness _____"; number_____; screen cloth material __
Shutters: ❑ hinged; ❑ fixed. Railing_____, Attic louvers _____
Exterior millwork: grade and species_____Paint _____; number coats_____
Additional information:_____

19. CABINETS AND INTERIOR DETAIL:
Kitchen cabinets, wall units: material __; lineal feet of shelves _____; shelf width _____
Base units: material_____; counter top _____; edging _____
Back and end splash_____ Finish of cabinets ____; number of coats _____
Medicine cabinets: make_____; model_____
Other cabinets and built-in furniture _____
Additional information:_____

20. STAIRS:

STAIR	TREADS Material/Thickness	RISERS Material/Thickness	STRINGS Material/Size	HANDRAIL Material/Size	BALUSTERS Materia/Size
Basement					
Main					
Attic					

Disappearing: make and model number _____
Additional information:_____

21. SPECIAL FLOORS AND WAINSCOT: (Describe Carpet as listed in Certified Products Directory)

FLOORS: LOCATION	MATERIAL, COLOR, BORDER, SIZES, GAGE, ETC.	THRESHOLD MATERIAL	WALL BASE MATERIAL	UNDERFLOOR MATERIAL
Kitchen				
Bath				

WAINSCOT: LOCATION	MATERIAL, COLOR, BORDER, SIZES, GAGE, ETC.	HEIGHT	HEIGHT OVER TUB	HEIGHT IN SHOWERS (FROM FLOOR)
Kitchen				
Bath				

Bathroom accessories: ☐ Recessed; material _____; number _____; ☐ Attached; material __; number __
Additional information: _____

22. PLUMBING:

FIXTURE	NUMBER	LOCATION	MAKE	MFR'S FIXTURE IDENTIFICATION NO.	SIZE	COLOR
Sink						
Lavatory						
Water Closet						
Bathtub						
Shower over tub○						
Stall shower○						
Laundry trays						

○☐ Curtain rod ○☐ Door ☐ Shower pan: material _____
Water Supply: ☐ public; ☐ community system; ☐ individual (private) system.★
Sewage disposal: ☐ public; ☐ community system; ☐ individual (private) system.★
★Show and describe individual system in complete detail in separate drawings and specifications according to requirements.
House drain (inside): ☐ cast iron; ☐ tile; ☐ other___House sewer (outside): ☐ cast iron; ☐ tile; ☐ other _____
Water piping: ☐ galvanized steel; ☐ copper tubing; ☐ other _____ Sill cocks, number _____
Domestic water heater: type _____; make and model ____; heating capacity _____
_____ gph. 100° rise. Storage tank: material _____; capacity _____ gallons.
Gas service: ☐ utility company; ☐ liq. pet. gas; ☐ other _____ Gas piping: ☐ cooking; ☐ house heating.
Footing drains connected to: ☐ storm sewer; ☐ sanitary sewer; ☐ dry well. Sump pump; make and model _____
_____; capacity _____; discharges into _____

23. HEATING:

☐ Hot Water. ☐ Steam. ☐ Vapor. ☐ One-pipe system. ☐ Two-pipe system.
☐ Radiators. _____ Convectors. ☐ Baseboard radiation. Make and model _____
Radiant panel: ☐ floor; ☐ wall; ☐ ceiling. Panel coil: material _____
☐ Circulator. ☐ Return pump. Make and model _____; capacity _____ gpm.
Boiler: maker and model _____ Output _____ Btuh.; net rating _____ Btuh.
Additional information: _____
Warm air: ☐ Gravity. ☐ Forced. Type of system _____
Duct material: supply; return _____ Insulation _____, thickness _____ ☐ Outside air intake.
Furnace: make and model_____ Input _____ Btuh.; output _____ Btuh.
Additional information: _____
☐ Space heater; ☐ floor furnace; ☐ wall heater. Input_____ Btuh.; output _____ Btuh.; number units ____
Make, model _____ Additional information: _____
Controls: make and types_____
Additional information: _____
Fuel: ☐ Coal; ☐ Oil; ☐ Gas; ☐ Liq. Pet. Gas; ☐ Electric; ☐ Other ____; storage capacity _____
Additional information: _____
Firing equipment furnished separately: ☐ Gas burner, conversion type. ☐ Stoker: hopper feed ☐; bin feed ☐
Oil burner: ☐ pressure atomizing; ☐ vaporizing_____
Make and model _____ Control _____

Additional information: _____

Electric heating system: type_____Input _____watts; @ _____volts; output _____ Btuh.

Additional information: _____

Ventilating equipment: attic fan, make and model_____; capacity _____ cfm.

kitchen exhaust fan, make and model_____

Other heating, ventilating, or cooling equipment_____

24. ELECTRIC WIRING:

Service: ☐ overhead; ☐ underground. Panel: ☐ fuse box; ☐ circuit-breaker; make _____AMP's _____

No. circuits_____

Wiring: ☐ conduit; ☐ armored cable; ☐ nonmetallic cable; ☐ knob and tube; ☐ other _____

Special outlets: ☐ range; ☐ water-heater; ☐ other _____

☐ Doorbell. ☐ Chimes. Push-button locations Additional Information:_____

25. LIGHTING FIXTURES:

Total number of fixtures_____Total allowance for fixtures, typical installation, $_____

Nontypical installation _____

Additional information:_____

26. INSULATION:

LOCATION	THICKNESS	MATERIAL, TYPE, AND METHOD OF INSTALLATION	VAPOR BARRIER
Roof			
Ceiling			
Wall			
Floor			

27. MISCELLANEOUS: *(Describe any main dwelling materials, equipment, or construction items not shown else-where; or use to provide additional information where the space provided was inadequate. Always references by item number to correspond to numbering used on this form.)*

_____

_____

_____

_____

_____

_____

_____

_____

HARDWARE: *(make, material, and finish.)*

_____

_____

SPECIAL EQUIPMENT: *(State material or make, model and quantity. Include only equipment and appliances which are acceptable by local law, custom and applicable FHA standards. Do not include items which, by estab-lished custom, are supplied by occupant and removed when he vacates premises or chattles prohibited by law from becoming realty.)*

_____

_____

_____

_____

_____

_____

_____

PORCHES:

_____
_____
_____
_____
_____
_____
_____
_____
_____
_____

TERRACES:

_____
_____
_____
_____
_____
_____
_____
_____
_____

GARAGES:

_____
_____
_____
_____
_____
_____
_____

WALKS AND DRIVEWAYS:
Driveway: width ____; base material _____; thickness _____"; surfacing material ____; thickness _____ ▪
Front walk: width ___; material ____; thickness ____". Service walk: width ____.; materila ____; thickness _____ ▪
Steps: material _____; treads _____"; risers _____". Check walls _____

OTHER ONSITE IMPROVEMENTS: *(Specify all exterior onsite improvements not described elsewhere, including items such as unusual grading, drainage structures, retaining walls, fence, railings, and accessory structures.)*

_____
_____
_____
_____
_____
_____
_____
_____
_____
_____
_____

LANDSCAPING, PLANTING, AND FINISH GRADING:
Topsoil_____" thick:☐ front yard; ☐ side yards;☐ rear yard to _____ feet behind main building.
Lawns (seeded, sodded, or sprigged): ☐ front yard _____; ☐ side yards _____; ☐ rear yard _____
Planting: ☐ as specified and shown on drawings; ☐ as follows:

_____Shade trees, deciduous, ____" caliper. Evergreen trees._____' to ____', B&B.
_____Low flowering trees, deciduous, ____' to __' _____Evergreen shrubs. _____' to ____', B&B
_____High-growing shrubs, deciduous ____' to __' _____Vines, 2-year _____
_____Medium-growing shrubs, deciduous, ___'to __' _____
_____Low-growing shrubs, deciduous, ___'to __' _____

IDENTIFICATION. This exhibit shall be identified by the signature of the builder, or sponsor, and/or the proposed mortgagor if the latter is known at the time of application.

Date _____   Signature _____

Signature _____

HUD-92005
VA Form 26-1852
Form FmHA 424-2
(6-79)
U.S. Government Printing Office: 1979 0 - 298-883

Chapter 5

Loan Closings

A loan closing is the final transaction of all the itemized expenditures and binding documents between the payor, or lending institution, and the payee, or borrower. There are many different types of loans which will have closings, but differ in the forms used and types of debits and credits entered, which total the bottom line figures. The three different types of closings I have included in this chapter are the types that you will experience if you borrow money to buy a lot, construct a house, and have a **mortgage** for the property.

The typical loan closing for either loan will generally be held in an attorney's office and will include forms, legal instruments, deeds, etc., that the attorney has prepared prior to the closing meeting. The lending institution will have given your attorney instructions as to what instruments, documents and information concerning the loan, that are to be used to consummate the loan closing. I will list for you what is generally included and expected from the borrower for each type of loan closing.

Number One: Loan Closing for a Lot Purchase Loan

— **Title Search** and Certificate of Title: A real estate **attorney** should be hired to perform a title search on a parcel of land prior to purchasing the property. This is a very important research process in which the attorney traces all the land owners back at least forty years. The attorney searches for flaws or defects in the wording of the deeds and for any liens or encumbrances that are against the property. After the attorney is sure the property is free of any encumbrances and clear of all defects, he or she will issue a certificate of title guaranteeing his search. This is paid for by the buyer and will generally cost about $300, unless the title search is very involved.

— **Survey** Plate: Banks require that a survey be performed on a parcel of land within six months prior to the time of purchase. If the seller's survey is not current, the buyer is generally expected to pay for the updated survey. This cost will usually be around $200, unless the parcel is large or has more than four sides.

— Deed or Title: Your real estate **attorney** will transfer the metes and bounds (location and dimensions) of the property from the survey plate to a new legal, binding document, called an instrument. The new instrument will also identify the parties that are transferring the property and specify the terms of payment and any conditions of the sale. The attorney's fee for preparing this instrument will be paid by the buyer and will vary from attorney to attorney. It really pays to shop around when seeking services of any kind.

— **Deed of Trust** or **Mortgage**. These are terms for a debt, lien or encumbrance against a parcel of property or any improvements that may be on the property, such a house. Whenever money is borrowed from a lending institution for the purpose of purchasing a parcel of land, there has to be a legal instrument drawn by a qualified attorney. The deed of trust or land mortgage will include the terms of financing between the lender and borrower, conditions, and a reference of the survey plate. By law this instrument of encumbrance must be recorded with the deed or title as a public record, until the debt is paid in full. Again, the cost for this preparation will vary and is paid by the buyer.

— Deed and Deed of Trust Recording Fee: These fees are paid by the buyer and are approximately $10 each.

— Tax Revenue Stamp. This is an excise tax imposed on the transfer of land. In North Carolina it is rated at $.50 per $500 of the amount paid. This is paid by the seller of the land.

Number Two: Loan Closing For A Construction Loan

A **construction loan** is a term loan, which means the money is loaned for a short period of time and is repaid in full at the end of the term of time. During the period the loan is available, interest is paid to the lender, usually monthly, on the amount of money that has actually been used. The closing will be very similar to the loan closing for a lot purchase, be held prior the release of the money loaned for construction, and will have the following items and cost for you the builder.

— The Deed or Title: Unless you are financially able to make a large substantial down payment, the lending institution will require the deed to your lot as collateral for your construction loan and as the down payment. Generally the appraisal of the lot should equal at least 10% of the amount of the construction loan in order for it to qualify as the down payment. It also has to be clear of any liens. The cost for this will have been part of the loan closing for a lot.

— An Appraisal of Your House Plans: An **appraisal** of your house plans will be an important part of the construction loan qualification. The bank you have selected will most likely have an appraisal company that they will send your house plans to. The appraisal company will do a thorough appraisal of your house plans and determine, based on several aspects, what your house will be worth once the construction is completed. This determines how much money you will be able to borrow to build your house. The cost of appraisal of house plans is approximately $250 to $300 and is paid by the borrower.

— **Builder's Risk Insurance** Policy: This is required to insure you, the builder, against all the potential hazards that could happen on a construction project.

— Foundation Survey or Plate: This is the **survey** which places the foundation of your house precisely on your lot. This survey will be due at the bank before you can make your first draw.

— **Loan Origination Fee**: As part of the construction loan closing, the lender will most likely require a 1% origination fee for processing your term construction loan. The 1% is 1% of the total loan amount that you pay at the closing. Ideally, it is advantageous if you can negotiate with the lender to have a combined construction **mortgage** loan. In this arrangement, you would pay the 1% origination fee only once, rather than for each type of loan. This situation would be ideal if the lender's mortgage rates are low. You should do a lot of checking with banks to try to get the very best deal available in your area.

— Attorney's Fee: The **attorney** that you have selected to process your closing will have all the closing costs itemized by line item, including his or her fee. My attorney's fee for our construction loan closing was $325.

— Interest: Any interest you owe on the construction loan for the last month of construction will be included in the loan closing for your mortgage.

Number Three: Loan Closing for a Mortgage

After you have completed the construction of your house, the inspector will do a final **inspection** and issue a certificate of occupancy if the house passes. The certificate of occupancy is given to your banker which attests that the house construction is completed and the construction loan is to be finalized.

The finalization of the construction loan means that it, being a term loan, must be paid in full. This is accomplished by the construction loan being paid off with a mortgage. The mortgage can be originated from the same bank that the construction loan was issued. This is known as a combination loan in which the construction loan is combined into a final mortgage.

This is certainly the simplest and least expensive way to have both loans, providing the bank's interest rates and terms for their final mortgages are comparable with other banks in your area.

The **mortgaging** bank, whether it is the same bank you have had your construction loan with or a different bank that you've selected, will issue to your attorney a statement of closing instructions. These instructions will be very similar to the instructions for a loan closing for the purchase of a parcel of land, but will include charges associated with a house, which is an improvement on the land. The following is a breakdown of the entries associated with a mortgage closing. The costs are variable.

— Pay off of the construction loan: The bank that you have negotiated with and selected will have all their terms, rates, conditions and monthly payments figured for your mortgage which will be used to pay off the construction loan.

— **Loan origination fee**: Unless you are able to have a combination loan, you will most likely have to pay an origination fee for the mortgage. The standard fee for this and construction loans is 1% of the amount borrowed (i.e., 1% of $90,000 = $900).

— Loan discount points: Banks offer discount points to make their loans more attractive. By paying for discount points at closing, you are simply buying down the rate of interest on the loan. Ex: You have shopped and found a bank that offers an interest rate that is 1/4% lower than the next lowest bank. They offer this lower rate with the assumption of 2 points. A point equals 1% of the loan amount and usually 1/8 of 1% of the interest rate.

— **Title Insurance** Premium: Title insurance may not be required in your transaction. If it is required, it is paid by the borrower. This insurance simply guarantees the bank payment of the mortgage in the event of any defects against the title or deed of the property that the house is built on. Any possible defects or encumbrances should be discovered in the attorney's title search. Title insurance premiums vary, but usually cost about $250 a year.

— Property Taxes: Tax on your lot and your new house will be prorated for the balance of the year and most likely added to your monthly mortgage payment. Your local tax office has formulas for figuring the amount of tax for your lot and house. If your lot and house is located within the city limits, you will probably be required to pay both city and county real estate tax.

— **Property Insurance**: Property Insurance is paid by the homeowner and is required by the lending institution when there is a mortgage. There are several different types of homeowner policies, such as basic, board and all risk. These three are the main types which cover the homeowner against fire, natural disasters, vandalism and theft. Another type of insurance that is important to consider is a liability policy which protects you, the homeowner, against loss from liability to third persons. Once you have selected an insurance company to cover your needs and have established a policy, the premium for the year will be prorated and, like your property taxes, included in your monthly mortgage payment. Some banks require that borrowers pay one full year's premium for insurance and a year's real estate tax in advance at the mortgage closing.

— **Private Mortgage Insurance**: Private mortgage insurance (P.M.I.) is required on conventional mortgage loans. This insurance insures the bank or mortgage company against default by the borrower for any reason. This insurance is required on mortgages in which the loan amount is 80% or more of the value of the property. Example: If your lot and new house has an appraised value of $100,000 and your mortgage amount is $75,000, you will not be required to have P.M.I. If your mortgage amount is $85,000, you will. P.M.I. is generally required for the first five years of the mortgage or until the amount of paid principle reduces the mortgage so that the ratio is 80% or less. The first year's P.M.I. is generally required to be paid in advance at the mortgage closing and usually costs approximately $300 per year. It is to be paid by the borrower.

— Final Survey Fee: The final **survey** is required to make sure that nothing on the property has changed since the pre-construction survey. This fee is to be paid at the mortgage closing by the borrower. The fee should be minimal since the survey that has previously been done is simply being checked for accuracy.

— Pest Inspection Fee: This is a wood-destroying insect inspector's report that a licensed company prepares and submits after they have sprayed for termites, etc. The cost for the spray application is approximately $100 and for the report approximately $50.

— **Attorney's Fee**: This will include his or her final charge which will include preparation of all legal instruments and mortgage documents.

— Recordation Fee of your Mortgage and Deed: This is a small fee of approximately $10 per document.

Chapter 6

Scheduling, Permits and Inspections

Well, if you have read this book to this chapter, you are either still very interested in building your own house or you are telling yourself, my, there is a lot more to building a house than I thought. You may even be overwhelmed with doubt. Take heart, be positive. If I did it, you can do it too! As stated before, you don't have to know how to build a set of kitchen cabinets, hang sheetrock or install a toilet fixture to be able to build a house. You just have to be good at planning, coordinating and managing money.

I want to review briefly what you should have accomplished once you reach this point. You have met with your attorney to discuss legalities and closings, with a clear deed, your lot is together, you know where your actual house site is to be located; you have thoroughly worked up your plans in detail; you have put together a line item total cost budget ledger; your house plans have been appraised; you have had a preconstruction survey performed; you have been given the go ahead by the bank for an approved construction loan; and you have opened up a separate checking account for the construction transactions. Before you can have any construction work performed on your lot, other than site preparation, you must have a **builder's permit**. I have included a sample permit on page 62. The city and county Inspector's Department will require a set of your house plans and a copy of the Health Department's permit. I have also included a local health department permit sample for your review on page 63. The inspector's office will charge you a fee for issuing your building permit. In our area of North Carolina, a permit costs approximately $10 per 100 square feet of house to be built. The Inspector's Office will send someone to your lot to post your building permit on a post that is visible from the street. Now you can jump up and down and begin contacting people to begin work on your project.

The **subcontractors** should call the inspectors to notify them when their phase of work is complete and ready for inspection. It's a good idea to follow up at the inspector's office to make sure the subcontractors are

62

PITT COUNTY, N.C.
INSPECTIONS DEPARTMENT

NOTICE

This Certifies that a Building Permit

has been issued to _____

for the erection of _____

Located at _____

Number _____   County Inspections Dept.

Date _____   By _____

THIS NOTICE MUST BE POSTED ON THE JOB BEFORE INSPECTIONS ARE MADE. PLACE POSTER ON A FLAT SURFACE (12" x15"), A MINIMUM OF FOUR (4) FEET IN HEIGHT. THIS NOTICE MUST BE VISIBLE FROM THE STREET.   830-6352

REQUIRED INSPECTION

BUILDING PRE SUB FLOOR _____
Slab _____
Footing _____
Framing _____
Insulation _____
Final _____

ELECTRICAL
Slab _____
Rough-in _____
Final _____

HEATING & A/C
Rough _____
Venting _____
Final _____

PLUMBING
Septic Tank _____
Slab _____
Sewer _____
Rough _____
Final _____

Building Permit Sample

_____ Suitable

_____ Provisionally Suitable

_____ Unsuitable

ENVIRONMENTAL HEALTH DIVISION

Existing _____

New _____

Repair _____

APPLICATION

Article 11 of Chapter 130A of The General Statutes of North Carolina

In Reply Please Refer To:

Date Received _____

Permit Number _____

Owner _____

Phone _____

Address _____ City _____ Zip _____

Subdivision Name _____ Lot No. _____ Block No. _____

Directions _____

_____

_____

Land Use _____ Bedrooms _____ Water Supply _____

Plot Plan Required: Yes _____ No _____

***This is an official document. Please retain with other valuable papers.

_____
Owner's Signature or Agent

IMPROVEMENT PERMIT

Site Classification Information:

Topography _____ Soil Texture _____

Soil Structure _____ Soil Depth _____

Restrictive Horizon: _____ Flood Plain _____

Soil Drainage: Internal _____ External _____

Other _____ Estimated Flow _____

Septic Tank Capacity _____

Nitrification Square Footage _____

Keep Rock _____ Inches from the natural soil surface.

Comments _____

_____

_____

_____

_____

_____

LAYOUT SKETCH

FRONT

Date Issued _____ By _____
Sanitarian

INSPECTION COMPLETED

Date _____ By _____
Sanitarian

White—OWNER'S COPY
Yellow—HEALTH DEPARTMENT COPY
Pink—BUILDING INSPECTOR'S COPY

VALID FOR 36 MONTHS

Health Department Permit Application Sample

calling in so as to keep your project on schedule.

The most important work you can do at this point is to write a schedule of events for the entire project. This is very important to keep you from pulling your hair out.

To give you a clear format of the overall scheduling of events, I have written out this list of scheduled events with notes and suggestions in the order that they are to be performed.

1. The grading sub will remove trees and build up the house site.
2. **Electricians** will place a temporary service pole and hook up to the utilities company. It is important that you require them to include a 220 volt receptacle at the temporary service pole.
3. The **Plumbing** Contractor will install a water meter and spigot. If your lot does not have access to city water and you will be using a well, call your well driller to put in the well for water service. There must be water at your house site at the very beginning before construction can actually start.
4. Building Supply Man: What you should do next is call to find out a delivery time on the brick and blocks needed for the foundation walls, piers and chimney. Sometimes bricks have to be ordered several weeks in advance depending on the style of brick that you choose.
5. **Porta-john** Company: Have a local porta-john company deliver a porta-john and begin a schedule for serving it.
6. **Footing** Contractor: Contact the footing contractor to give him the go ahead for digging and pouring the footings. **He must call for an inspection of the footing trenches before they are poured.**
7. Mason: Schedule him to start as soon as the concrete **footings** have dried and cured for at least two days. He will begin laying the bricks and blocks for the walls and piers
8. Building Inspector's Office: Two weeks after the **footings** are dug and poured, the masonry contractor should be finishing up with the foundation. This is the time that the **building inspector's** office should be notified that the footings and **foundations** are completed and need to be inspected as soon as possible.
9. **Trash Container Company:** This is also a good time to schedule a trash container company to deliver a dumpster to the house site once the masonry work is completed. If you have your own truck you can save money by hauling your own trash. Subcontractors generally don't clean up behind themselves. The project goes much better if the construction debris is cleaned up each week, or at least every two weeks.

Note: After the **foundations** and footings are inspected you should have a tandem dump truck bring a couple of loads of sand to your construction site. The sand should be put inside the foundation walls either by front-end loader or by hand. The sand provides a good grade under your house and will be good for future subcontractors to crawl around on while they are doing work under your house. After the sand is in place, put down a layer of plastic which will serve as a **moisture barrier.**

10. **Framing** Subcontractor: You are now ready for a very exciting part of the project, called framing. Your framing **subcontractor** should have the floor joist boards and wall studs delivered, so his crew can begin building a floor on the foundation. The framing of the floors, vertical walls, building of the roof, mounting of the windows and exterior doors, and the nailing of the insulation sheathing to the exterior of the house, and the nailing of roofing felt paper to the roof, is called drying in. This process should be completed in two weeks or less after the foundation has been inspected.

11. Inspector's Office: As soon as the framing process called drying in is complete, the inspector's office should be notified again for a framing **inspection.** It is important to make sure these inspectors are called just as soon as the work is completed so that they can do a timely inspection and not hold up the work process.

12. Mason: If your house plan calls for a fireplace, schedule your mason to build the fireplace and run the chimney up after the house has been framed and dried in. The framers should be finishing up with the exterior boxing at this time also.

13. Mechanical Subcontractor Rough-ins: The next phase of construction work to be performed is called the mechanical **subcontractor** rough-ins. The first subcontractor to begin in this stage is the **plumber,** who will cut out and drill holes in the walls, the wall bases, and roof to run the drain and water lines throughout the house.

14. Heating and Air Conditioning Installation Company: The next subcontractors to follow will be the **heating and air conditioning** installation company. They will begin to run the duct work and establish where the heating and cooling units will go. It is a good idea to meet with them to help place the floor vents in each room.

15. **Electricians:** Your project is now ready for the electricians. They should be the last rough-in because you want to lessen the chance of nicking any wires that are being installed. Be sure to spend a lot of time with them to ensure that all the receptacles, switches, fixtures and telephone jacks are in the right places. If you have to have a septic tank at your lot, this is a good time to have it installed.

16. Inspector's Office: Now that the mechanical subcontractors have completed their rough-ins, the inspector's office is notified, so they can make another **inspection** of all of the mechanical rough-ins during one trip. They have to approve the house at this point before insulation can be installed.

    Let's review briefly where we are, to help with the total scheduling. We allow a week for the footings to be dug; a week for the foundation to be finished; two weeks for framing; a week for plumbing rough-in; a week for heating and air conditioning rough-in; and a week for electrical rough-in. To be safe, let's add two weeks to this schedule in case of inclement weather, or other delays that can occur. We are nine weeks into the project at this point.

17. After the mechanical rough-in inspections have passed, shingles and flashings should be put on the roof. This is also the time for exterior veneer (brick, wood siding, masonite or vinyl siding, etc.), to begin being installed.

18. Insulation Company: While this type of work is happening on the outside of the house, the **insulation** company can begin insulating throughout the inside of your house. Once the insulation company has finished, the energy services department of your utilities company will need to be notified for an inspection, if you are qualified for the **E-300** program.

19. Inspector's Office: As soon as the insulation company has finished, they should call the inspector's office to schedule the insulation inspection.

20. **Sheetrock.** All the moving of receptacles, etc., should be finished at this point, because your house is now ready for sheetrock. Once the sheetrock is installed, the ceiling sprayed and the wall joints finished with compound, you'll be thinking, wow, we are about finished with this house. You can really get excited at this point, and you should, but there is still a lot of work to be done. Let's allow four more weeks to our schedule for the shingle work, outside veneer, insulation, and sheetrock finishing. You can breathe a little easier now. Your house is a little over 50 percent completed, and it's really starting to look good as you walk from room to room. The project has come a long way fast, but progress now is going to seem to be at a snail's pace, even though the weather is not as great a factor when inside work is begun.

21. Finish Carpenter and Crew: At this point in time, you should be starting week number 14. Your finish carpenter and crew should be ready to set up shop in your house. They will be working for several weeks

if they are doing all of the trim and cabinets. They will start by putting the plywood floor over the subfloor and installing hardwood flooring if it's required in your floor plan. Once the flooring is in, they can begin mounting the interior doors throughout the house, casing windows and doors, building mantles, cabinets, vanities, shelving, cutting and fastening moldings and installing a staircase if there's one for your plans. This is all detailed work and takes time to do it right.

22. Vinyl Flooring Installers: If your house has any tile or vinyl flooring in it, it is time for the tile and vinyl to be installed. The trim carpenter will have plenty to do and will be able to work around wherever the tile is being installed.

23. Cement Finishers: On the outside during this phase, the concrete should be poured and finished for the driveway, carport, walks, and stoops. Also, the exterior painting can begin. You should allow at least five weeks for all the trim carpentry work, tile and concrete work to be completed.

Approximately at this point on the schedule, you should be starting week number 19. Your project has come a long way and you are now ready to begin finishing up.

24. **Painting** Company: After all the trim carpentry is finished, have your painting company begin painting and staining the whole interior. Allow two weeks for them.

25. **Wallpaper** Hangers: As soon as the painters have finished rooms that wallpaper is going in, have the wallpaper hangers begin their work.

26. **Plumbing** Company: After vinyl or tile flooring is installed in the bathrooms, the plumbers should return to install the toilets and all other fixtures. Be sure to stress to them the importance of being extremely careful on the finished flooring.

27. **Heating and Cooling** Company: The heating and cooling company should be notified at this time to bring the units out to your house and begin installing them. The mechanics will be outside and under the house most of the time and out of the painters' and wallpaper hangers' way.

28. **Electrical** Company: Once all the walls are painted and wallpaper is on them, have the electrical company bring the fixtures you picked out previously and install them.

29. **Landscape** Contractor: While this is going on, have your landscaper begin backfilling and rough grading the yard. This is also the time to have decks built. I recommend that wherever you are planning to

build a deck, you have the landscaper backgrade and smooth out the dirt before the deck building process begins. This will ensure that you will have good grade and drainage under your deck and not water standing after heavy rains.

30. Appliance Store: After the electricians are finished, have the appliance store deliver your appliances and have the plumbing company bring the fixtures you picked out to be installed. The appliances should be there before the plumbers so that they can hook up the ice maker, dishwasher, etc. While the plumbers are finishing up on the inside and trenching a water line from the meter to the house on the outside, have the landscaper finish grading, seeding, and planting shrubs and trees, etc.

To estimate where we are on the schedule, let's allow two weeks for painting, staining and wallpaper hanging, and three weeks for all mechanical fixture completion, landscaping and appliance installation. If you're on schedule, you should be approximately starting week number 24. This is what is known on a project as the short rows, where you really see the end in sight.

All that is left at this point is cleaning throughout thoroughly, touch-up painting and carpet installation.

Once the carpet is installed you are ready to call the **inspector** for the final inspection. The inspector will do a walk-through inspection to make sure that everything in your house project is completed as it should be. The inspector will issue a certificate of occupancy which will ensure your banker that the house is completed. Some bankers may want to join the inspector on the final walk-through, others may not.

You will need a **surveyor** to do a final survey on your lot and house site. He will need to submit to you the survey plates that will be required at the bank for the **closing**. The last business to settle before you begin moving into your new home is the closing. The bank that has your construction loan could also be the bank that has your mortgage. Sometimes banks are willing to do both and call it a combination loan, which can save you money by not having to pay some of the closing expenses twice. Please refer back to Chapter Five, Loan Closings, for additional information on closings. The closing will most likely be at an attorney's office and your banker will probably not be there. Your **attorney** is responsible for making sure that all the paperwork concerning the deed to your lot and your mortgage is in order. All of this information must be recorded and all of the monies that are to be paid or collected must be completed at this time so that the entire project is finalized.

This can be a rather nerve-racking experience because of the great sums of money that you are signing your name to. Prepare yourself to sign your name many, many times. The good thing is once it's over, it's over and you can enjoy moving into your new home and experience all the excitement and happiness that goes with it.

SECTION TWO

Construction Work, Description and Terminology

I have written this section in conjunction with the previous chapter to help you to have a better understanding of the actual fundamental work process of each phase of the construction project. The order of each description parallels the schedule of events in the previous chapter. Defining the terminology will help you when you talk to subcontractors and basically everyone involved in the construction process. This section contains helpful hints to make your project progress smoother and make your final result more attractive.

Chapter 7

Site Preparation

If your lot has been surveyed within six months prior to construction start-up, it should be O.K. to begin lot grading. If there hasn't been a survey on the lot within that time, be sure to hire a **surveyor** to ascertain that dimensions and corner posts are accurate. When you negotiate a fee with the surveyor, tell him you will need him for two more surveys: the foundation plot survey and the final survey. Size up your lot to see what it really needs before you begin doing anything. People who buy lots in the country that aren't on a community waste system should spend some time with a Health Department representative to consider where to put the **septic tank** and lines. This will help determine where the house and driveway will be placed on the lot. Once it is established, trees can be marked for removal if your lot is wooded. After the trees are removed and the house site cleared, fill sand or dirt should be brought in to build up the house site about 4 to 6 inches above the original grade level. It's very important not to build your house in a hole, unless you are building a house with a basement. People who have cleared lots should have the grading contractor leave the house site high and grade from the house site to the lot property lines to ensure proper drainage. This will help the **landscape** contractor to be able to do a better job when it's time for him to landscape the yard.

Once the house site and lot has been graded, the surveyor should survey and place stakes where the actual house site is to be. It is very important that you check behind the surveyor and refer back to the Health Department permit to make sure that your house site is located in exactly the place that it should be. This is especially true if you are required to have a septic tank.

Chapter 8

Footings

Footings are trenches and holes that have been excavated and filled with concrete. The person responsible for digging and pouring the footings will use a transit and rod to ensure accuracy as he lays out the dimensions of the house perimeter walls. He will build a temporary frame made of two-by-fours, outside of the perimeter lines. This frame is called "batter boards" and is used to connect mason's twine. The twine is pulled from frame to frame to outline where the perimeter footings and the foundation pier footings will be excavated. After the measurements have been double checked, he is ready to mark the ground with lime or paint so as to have clear lines to follow as he is digging.

Footings can be dug by hand, but in most places today they are being dug by small backhoe tractors. Once the footings are dug, the digger prepares the trenches and holes for the concrete to be poured. The standard footing trench for a house in our area is 16 inches wide and 8 inches deep. I had ours dug 20 inches wide because our house has two stories and I wanted to make sure the footing wouldn't crack from the weight. It is not always required by code but it is important, I feel, to have steel reinforcing rods, called rebar, placed in the footing trench. Number 8 rebar, which is one-half inch in diameter, is adequate. This will hold the footing together even if there is some settling and a possible crack. The person placing the rebar in the trench should elevate it with rod chairs so that it is approximately half the distance from the bottom of the trench to the top of where the concrete level will be. Footings should be set below the frost line. Before the footings are poured, they should be inspected by someone from the **inspector's office**. The best concrete to use is ready-mixed concrete. It is delivered to your house site and is sold by the yard. Make sure if your house plans include a fireplace and chimney that the footing base is at least a foot wider than the chimney width. The footings should cure or dry at least two days before the foundation work begins.

Chapter 9

Foundations

The **foundation** is the part of the house that is cemented to the footings and is used to build the floors onto. There are several factors to consider when deciding on the type of foundation for your house; such as, if your design has a basement, the soil conditions of your lot, structural design of your house, and the water table depth. If you are building a house with a basement, be sure that the masonry **subcontractor** has built basement walls before and is familiar with proper drainage and waterproofing. Basement building will require detailed planning while you are in the design and planning stage. I like basements and wanted to include one in our design, but the water table here is too high and the land is too flat to be approved by the Inspector's Office for a basement.

There are two main types of foundations: the strip type and the slab type. The strip type is the most common and consists of a poured concrete footing that has vertical block walls or a vertical poured concrete wall. Most strip foundations are made of eight-inch cement blocks. The block foundation is less expensive than the solid poured concrete foundation wall, but the concrete wall foundation is stronger.

The strip foundation type, along with having vertical perimeter walls, has vertical piers at specific load bearing points that are used for support under the first floor. See the illustration for footings and foundations on page 79 to get a better visual of this type of foundation. The piers support the floor joists and girders on which the flooring is nailed.

The slab foundation is a solid concrete floor and can be poured on top of the ground or on top of a cement block foundation that has been filled in with sand. This type of foundation is more commonly used in moderate climates and for one story houses, apartment complexes and commercial projects. The raised slab is poured on top of compacted sand that is filled inside the cement block foundation walls. The plumbing, water lines and drainage lines have to be roughed in and placed before the slab is poured. After the rough-in, the sand is compacted with tapping machines, the exterminator sprays chemicals, and a **vapor barrier** is put down. Four-inch square reinforcement wire is placed on top of the vapor barrier. This gives strength to the concrete. Now the slab area is ready to be poured and finished.

There are a couple of other **foundation** types. Pressure treated wood foundations are becoming more popular in extremely cold climate areas. It is not recommended to pour concrete when the temperature is 32°F or colder. The plywood and stud foundations are also much easier to insulate than the masonry types.

The fourth type of foundation is the pile supported foundation. This is the type of foundation that beach cottages are built on in coastal areas. After any foundation is completed, the inspector's office should be called to do a thorough foundation inspection.

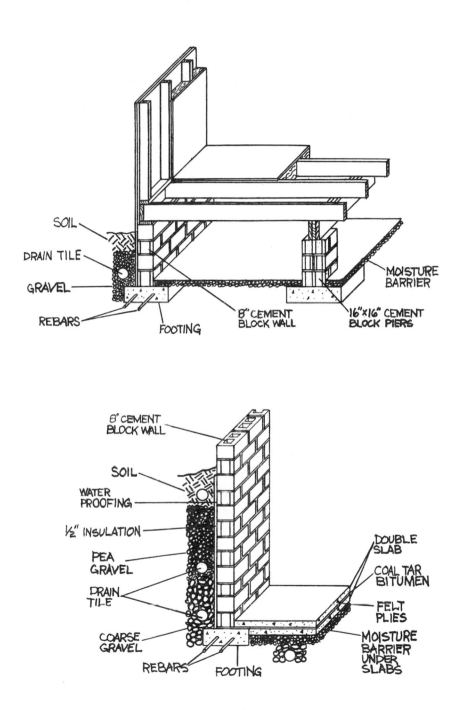

SOIL

DRAIN TILE

GRAVEL

REBARS

FOOTING

8" CEMENT BLOCK WALL

16"x16" CEMENT BLOCK PIERS

MOISTURE BARRIER

8" CEMENT BLOCK WALL

SOIL

WATER PROOFING

½" INSULATION

PEA GRAVEL

DRAIN TILE

COARSE GRAVEL

REBARS

FOOTING

DOUBLE SLAB

COAL TAR BITUMEN

FELT PLIES

MOISTURE BARRIER UNDER SLABS

Footings Foundations

Chapter 10

Framing

The frame is the skeleton of a building that provides the structural strength for the floor, walls and roof. It is very important that the framing be consistently in line and concise in order to provide straight, flat walls, level floors and square corners. There are several types of framing and a variety of framing materials. The most common style of residential framing is wood platform framing. This method uses smaller sizes of lumber compared to post and beam type framing, which uses heavy, large sizes of lumber.

There are many species of coniferous trees that framing lumber is made from. The Douglas fir, hemlock and pine are the most common. These woods are lightweight, yet strong, and are milled to any size board you will need.

You will have the quantity of the different sizes of boards needed for framing your house from the materials list that you requested either from your building supply estimator, or the person who drew your plans, or your framer. Framing lumber has been planed smooth on all four sides. The actual dimensions of the boards has been decreased because of the planing and kiln drying process. For an example, a 2-inch by 4-inch stud board is really 1½ inches by 3½ inches by the standard 93 inches in length. Framing lumber should not have a higher moisture content than 15%. This helps prevent warping and shrinking as the wood continues to dry over time. Lumber is graded to determine the number of defects. The materials list should specify the grade of lumber to be used for each part of the framing.

An example of a wall framing **stud** is number one grade, meaning it is straight, has uniform density with a minimum, tolerable number of knots. Your framer will be familiar with the grades used in your area.

Aside from boards, you will be buying sheathing material for floors, roofs, and exterior walls. The most common type of sheathing material is plywood, which comes in many types and thicknesses, but there are other types of sheathing such as wafer board, fibre board and exterior pressed panels. The materials list will include the different types and sizes of sheathing needed for each application of the framing process.

If you are not able to be on your lot to inspect the lumber when it is delivered, have the framing subcontractor inspect it for you. If there is a large number of warped and undesirable boards, don't accept the delivery. There will always be a few boards that shouldn't be used for framing, but they can be used for bracing, spacer blocks, etc.

As your framing materials are delivered to the job site, coordinate with your framing subcontractor to determine a designated area to place the materials. You want them to be close to the house but not so close that they are in the way. Have the deliverymen place the materials on pallets or two-by-fours in order to keep the lumber from being on the ground. Always be sure that unused lumber is wrapped with plastic or tarps at the end of each work day.

The framing crew will begin by cutting either two-by-six or two-by-eight pressure treated boards into the right lengths to fit over the exterior foundation walls. These boards are called sills and, depending on the code in your area, are either one or two layers thick. The lumber used for sills has to be pressure treated in order to be rot resistant. In some areas a termite shield is required. This shield is simply light gauge sheet metal or flashing aluminum material that is cut and placed on the top of the foundation wall prior to the placement of the sill. The sill is attached to the foundation wall with anchor bolts that are set in concrete. Please refer to the floor frame diagram on the facing page.

One of the **E-300** requirements is that there be foam sealer or caulking put on the top of the foundation wall prior to the sill. This sealer will minimize cold air infiltration.

Once the framers have finished with the sills, they will cut shim blocks to put on the top of the foundation piers. These will ensure that the floor will be level. The framers will study the plans and determine where they need to put girders to give the most support for load bearing walls. A girder is two or three boards that are the same size as the floor joists nailed together which make a thick, heavy beam. Girders are stood up vertically (on their narrow edge) on top of the foundation piers and are used where the span between walls is too great for an uninterrupted run of floor joists. Floor joists are the stout, heavy boards that support the floor and interior vertical walls. Your architect or draftsman will determine the size of joists needed based on the distance they span between the foundation walls and the pier supports. The framers will cut and nail up a joist header, which is a joist board that is turned up on its narrow side and placed on top of the sill running with the perimeter of

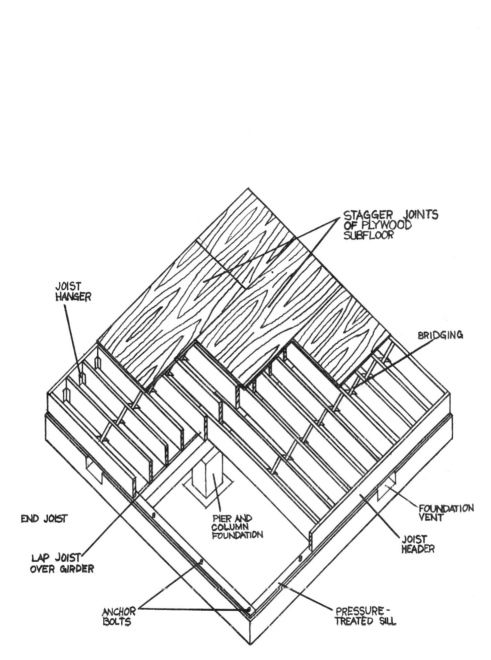

STAGGER JOINTS
OF PLYWOOD
SUBFLOOR

JOIST
HANGER

BRIDGING

END JOIST

PIER AND
COLUMN
FOUNDATION

FOUNDATION
VENT

JOIST
HEADER

LAP JOIST
OVER GIRDER

ANCHOR
BOLTS

PRESSURE-
TREATED SILL

Floor Frame Diagram

the exterior wall. The joist header is run all the way around the perimeter on top of the sill. The floor joists are butted up against and nailed to this header. Building codes vary, but in general the floor joists should be placed on 16-inch centers, have joist hangers for extra support, lap over the girders, and have bridging between the joist at the point that is half of the joist length for stability and to prevent squeaking.

Now that the main support structure of the floor frame is in place, the framers are ready to put down the subfloor sheathing. Subfloor sheathing is four-by-eight sheets of plywood that are available from one-half inch to one inch thick, depending on your specifications and how much you want to spend. The plywood should be approved by the American Plywood Association. The subfloor provides the base for the finished floor. The framers should stagger the joints of the plywood, use contact construction adhesive on each floor joist and allow about 1/32 of an inch between each sheet butt joint, to allow for expansion and contraction.

The framing is about to have a vertical look at this point, now that the floor frame and subfloor are in place. (See Wall Frame illustration on facing page.) Vertical walls for many years have been the standard four inch thickness. Due to the recent emphasis that has been put on energy efficiency, thicker walls are acceptable. Architects and builders are using 2-inch by 6-inch studs for exterior walls rather than 2-inch by 4-inch studs. This allows more space for more insulation which will produce a higher R factor for the walls. The building code for 2-inch by 6-inch framing should be 24-inch centers.

Since the spacing is 24-inch instead of 16-inch on centers for the standard two-by-four inch wall studs, there is less pieces of lumber used, but 2-inch by 6-inch studs cost more, so the cost for the, exterior wall studs is about the same. Your architect or **draftsman** will be helpful in deciding which you should choose, considering the climate of where you are building. I chose 2-inch by 4-inch wall studs, because the climate in eastern North Carolina is moderate and 2-inch by 6-inch walls require special furring for finishing out the windows and doors.

A standard wall stud is a planed down 2-inch by 4-inch board that is 93 inches long. This precut board is the right length to make an eight foot wall section once it has been nailed between a 2-inch by 4-inch sole or base plate and two thicknesses of 2-inch by 4-inch boards, which make the top plate.

A trend in some styles of housing is to have 9 or 10-foot ceilings rather than the standard 8-foot. This adds to the looks of a room, and is a must if your plans call for circle top windows, but it really increases the

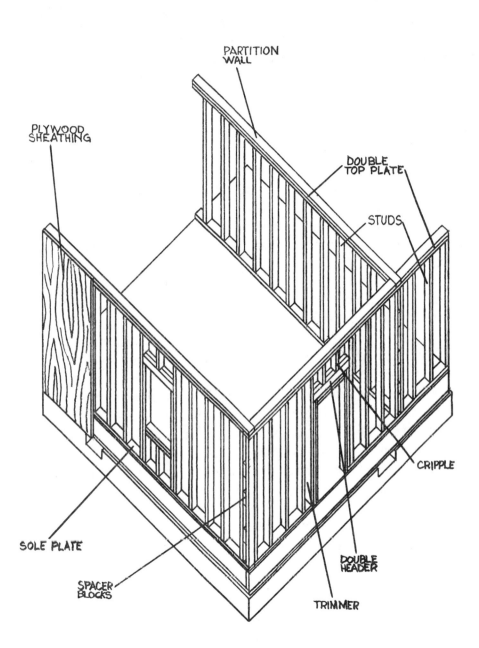

PARTITION WALL

PLYWOOD SHEATHING

DOUBLE TOP PLATE

STUDS

CRIPPLE

SOLE PLATE

SPACER BLOCKS

DOUBLE HEADER

TRIMMER

Wall Frame Illustration

cost of the house. Generally, any time you deviate from standard design it costs more in building.

The framers will study the floor plans and begin cutting and nailing together the boards to make the interior and exterior walls. They will allow for the openings of the windows and doors. As they construct a wall section, they must put headers above the windows and door openings.

The header is usually a 2-inch by 6-inch or 2-inch by 8-inch board cut to the length of the windows and door frame. This header above the openings distributes the load bearing weight to each side. Once a wall section is framed, it is stood upright and placed on top of the subfloor within the chalk lines that are used to assure the accuracy of the wall placement. Corners are made of three studs and short blocks, called spacers, cut to the width of the studs, that are used for strength and to provide a surface for nailing on the interior and exterior finishings of the walls. Exterior walls that join together to make corners have to be thoroughly braced. There are several code approved ways to accomplish this. The most popular in our area is using exterior grade plywood on each side of the corners.

After the framers have placed and braced all of the vertical walls, they will begin framing the roof. See the roof frame illustration on the facing page. You have two choices with the roof framing. You can select prefabricated roof **trusses** or have the framers stick-build your roof using rafters, ridge boards and roof joists. Consult your architect or draftsman for which would be better for your house plan. If either can be used, the cost of using prefab trusses is less and goes up a lot faster. One factor that can drive up the cost of using trusses, though, is if your roof design calls for trusses that are so large that a crane has to be used in order to place them. Something else to consider is that you lose a considerable amount of usable headroom space in the attic by using prefab trusses. The inspectors that inspect your project, should do a thorough job on the roof framing **inspection**. If you choose stick frame building, the rafters should be nailed with the bow of the boards up; whenever there is a skylight or chimney, the rafters should be doubled; there should be a 2-inch air space between the roof frame and the chimney; and the roof framing should allow for code approved ventilation, either gable vents, ridge and soffit vents or a combination of all three.

In most cases, APA approved plywood is used for roof sheathing. If your plans call for a vaulted ceiling and exposed beams, there are several combinations of materials that can be used. The roof plywood sheathing should be at least one-half inch thick and put down so the joints are stag-

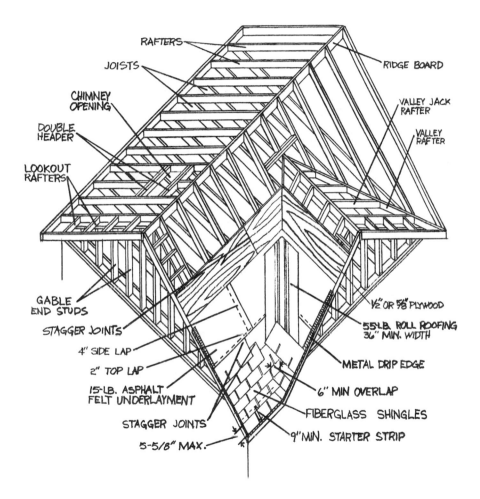

RAFTERS

JOISTS

CHIMNEY OPENING

DOUBLE HEADER

LOOKOUT RAFTERS

GABLE END STUDS

STAGGER JOINTS

4" SIDE LAP

2" TOP LAP

15-LB. ASPHALT FELT UNDERLAYMENT

STAGGER JOINTS

5-5/8" MAX.

RIDGE BOARD

VALLEY JACK RAFTER

VALLEY RAFTER

1/2" OR 5/8" PLYWOOD

55 LB. ROLL ROOFING 36" MIN. WIDTH

METAL DRIP EDGE

6" MIN OVERLAP

FIBERGLASS SHINGLES

9" MIN. STARTER STRIP

Roof Frame Illustration

gered like the subfloor. As soon as the roof sheathing is nailed down, it should be covered with black felt roofing paper. This will dry in the structure and will be adequate until the shingles can be put on. Most framing crews are multi-talented and are willing to put the shingles on the roof and do the flashing work for a better price than a roofing company. Shingles can't be put on until the chimney and plumbing rough-in work is finished.

After the framers are finished with the felt paper, they are ready to begin installing all the exterior windows and doors. Be sure to have the framing supervisor check each window and door carefully when they are delivered, to be sure they are what your plans call for and that there is no damage. Once the exterior doors and windows are installed, your house will be at a point of completion that is known as being dried-in. This will be very exciting as the house is really taking shape. Drying-in should go up quickly. Our house of 3,650 square feet under roof went from a completed foundation to a complete dry-in, which was stick-built, in a total of seven working days.

Boxing the roof eaves is usually a separately bid part of the finishing of the exterior that the framers do. You should be sure to discuss this with the framing subcontractor when discussing a price quotation prior to the beginning of construction. The boxing gives the roof ends of your house a finished look. The boxing also accommodates the ventilation of the roof and attic. Boxing consists of a facia board which is usually a number one grade, 1-inch by 6-inch board that is nailed against the butt ends of the rafters or trusses. Underneath the eaves, plywood (usually one-fourth inch thick) is ripped to fit the eaves and then nailed up. This is where the space for the roof vents are cut out and installed. Usually, boxing cannot be done until after the exterior siding is completed. The original framing crew will return to do the boxing. This is done toward the end of your project when they are also doing things like building decks, putting up porch rails and pickets or finishing a garage. Be sure to be specific with the framing subcontractor when getting prices on all these different types of work that his crew will be performing.

After the house is framed and is dried-in, call the **inspector's** office to have it inspected. They should be there within two days' time. One thing that the inspector may miss that is important to look for, is studs that are out of line. I have wished many times that I had gone from wall to wall checking for warped studs or studs that were simply not nailed in line. Studs that are out of line will cause a bow in the sheetrock once it is nailed up. Even in the most expensive houses, there will be some bowing due to the studs twisting or warping naturally in the drying process. This can't be helped, just as over a period of time nails or screws will sometimes be pushed out by the continued drying of the lumber. These factors don't occur a lot, so don't be alarmed. You can check for out of line studs by simply taking a length of masonry line and with someone's help, pull the line from corner to corner on each wall throughout your newly framed house. Once you have discovered the out of line studs, mark them and have the framers either adjust them or replace them. This will make your sheetrock work finish out much flatter and have a more professional look.

As soon as your house has passed the framing inspection, you are ready to contact the mechanical **subcontractors** to coordinate their rough-in work so that you can stay on schedule. While the mechanical contractors are doing the rough-in of their systems, you can have your mason return to your house and begin work on the fireplace and chimney. The hearth should have clean, consistent mortar joints. You may want to consider some decorative bricks for the edge of the hearth. The round edge type are called bull nose bricks. Have your building supply salesperson show you all the different varieties of bricks available for hearths and for porch steps. These are things you can decide on in the early planning stages that can enhance the decor of your house.

Chapter 11

Mechanical Systems

Much of the critical planning and scheduling of your house construction involves the installation of plumbing, electrical and heating and air conditioning systems, which are known as the mechanical systems. The framers should have studied the house plans and framed the house so as to avoid putting a floor joist in line where a toilet fixture is to go. At best, there will have to be modifications throughout the mechanical rough-ins. The key to having a professional job is to make sure that the subcontractors do neat and accurate work. This stage of the construction is where being your own contractor really pays off. The building inspectors will make sure that all the work meets the required standards of the codes. There are little things that he's likely to overlook. Your insistence on quality and your active involvement will ensure that annoying little problems will be avoided.

The mechanical subcontractors will be responsible for getting their own permits and calling for inspectors once they have completed a stage of their system. I found it very helpful and important to have a good rapport with the inspector's office so that I could call to check on the subcontractors to make sure that they were doing what they were saying they were doing. It is important to stay on top of each stage of the project. By communicating with the inspector's office, it will help you to coordinate your upcoming **subcontractors** and **inspections**. This will help you to stay on schedule. You will want the subs to go in and out, one after the other.

Chapter 12

Plumbing

The first mechanical **subcontractor** to begin after framing has been inspected is the plumbing company. The plumbers have to do a lot of drilling and cutting through the floors, wall studs and the roof in order to rough-in all the water line, drain pipe and vents. They will actually come to your house in three stages and at three different times. The first trip will be to trench and run a water line from the existing main line that runs in front of your house, whether your house is being built on a city lot or a lot that is in a community water system district. If your lot is in the country and you are planning to use a well, the well installation should be one of the first things on your list to have done. The plumbers will stub up a short piece of pipe and put a spigot on it. There must be water and electricity on your lot before the mason can begin laying the foundation on top of the footings.

The second stage of work which the plumbers will come to your house and begin is called the rough-in stage. See the plumbing rough-in illustration on the next page. The plumbers begin by cutting and fitting together the sewer main under your house. This line is usually four inches in diameter and is either ABS plastic or cast iron. Cast iron is now almost obsolete except on commercial and industrial projects. The sewer and gray water drains should have a slope of at least 1/16 inch per foot but no more than 1/4 inch per foot of the length.

After the plumbers have completed the drain and sewer line system under your house, they will begin drilling holes through the floor where the walls are, to begin bringing in the drain lines into the baths, kitchen, etc. At this point the lines have been reduced from 4-inch sewer line to 3-inch and then to 2-inch coming through the base plates of the floor. Lavatories, sinks and tubs are reduced further to one to one-half inches. The toilet is a 3-inch drain with a flange that fits approximately one inch above the subfloor to allow for the finished floor. As the plumbers are fitting the drain pipe together, they will be tying it in to vent pipes, which go up through the attic and through the roof of your house. That's what

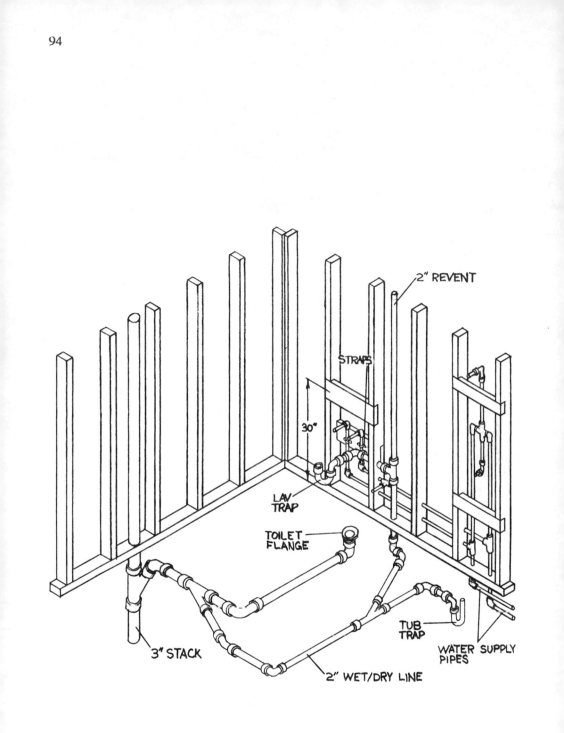

Plumbing Rough-in

those strange pipes are that you may have wondered about all these years. There have to be vents in order for water to flow properly. Make sure your house design has the vent stacks on the back roof section of your house.

Plumbing crews usually work in teams. While one is running the drain line systems, another will be putting together the water line system. Again, this work starts under the house and progresses up through the floors and walls. The plumber will cap off the water line near the water supply line in order to test the systems.

Water line materials have progressed over the years like all other building materials. The three most commonly used materials today for water lines are copper, PVC, and polybutalaine. Polybutalaine is the newest, easiest to install, least expensive and is a lot less susceptible to freezing than the other materials. Copper is the most expensive and takes the longest to install, as the joints and fittings have to be heated and soldered together. I see no advantage in using copper. I chose polybutalaine.

This is also the time when the plumbers will bring in the fiberglass shower and tub units, if your plans call for them. They do it at this time because often they have to remove studs in order to fit them into the bathrooms.

Once all of the plumbing systems are roughed in, you need to do a close inspection to make sure that each fixture is lining up on the wall exactly where it should be. Measure all of your toilet, laboratory, sink, tub, shower, washer and hot water heater drain and water lines to ensure they are correctly placed. Again, you being the contractor pays off. If it's not where it should be, have it moved. If you don't and it passes inspection, the next thing you know it will have sheetrock around it.

Other things to look for besides correct placement are the drain and water lines being properly secured with straps and hangers. The water lines will be under approximately 45 pounds of pressure and should be secure throughout the system in order to avoid vibration (which is called hammering) that is caused when fixtures are quickly turned off.

Another important area to check is where the plumbers have had to cut through a base plate, a joist or a wall stud. They should have nailed a piece of sheet metal across any holes that they have made that are significantly larger than the pipe that goes through the hole. Be sure that the plumbers, the electricians and the heating and cooling system installers do this in order to prevent mice and insects from having access into your new home.

The plumbers will put both the drain and water line systems under pressure to ensure that there are no leaks. While the systems are under pressure, the inspector will be called out to do the inspection. Once the inspection is approved, the plumbers are finished until stage 3, which is installing the fixtures and line hookups. The fixtures which are the lavatories, kitchen sink, toilets, tubs and showers, and hot water heaters are installed toward the end of the project after the finished carpentry is completed.

You can spend a lot of money on plumbing fixtures. The manufacturers have catered to the whims of every design and contemporary taste. Whatever you want in color, style and application is available to you. It's important to make your selection of fixtures and really everything in the line of finishings for your house as soon as possible prior to construction. Don't get caught in a situation where it's time to install the lavatories and toilets and you and your spouse are running all over town, frantically going nuts because you can't decide which color goes best with the wallpaper that you have selected. Be decisive and plan way ahead.

There are a couple of tips I want to share with you concerning the plumbers finishing up. Check the caulking around the kitchen sink and lavatories, to make sure that there is a good seal and that it looks neat. It's also a good idea to check the toilets to make certain that they are securely bolted to the floor. The plumbers will be trenching from the water meter to the main water line under your house in order to connect your house system with the existing water system. They should tap and pack the dirt that they put back into the trench, so that there won't be a lot of settling which will make a low place in your yard.

Once the plumbing rough-in is completed, you can contact whoever is putting the shingles on your roof (if your roof has shingles) and have them start on finishing the roof. Make sure that they do a good job of cutting and installing the flashing around the chimney, using masonry nails and flashing cement. They will use a special type of pipe flashing that will fit snugly and securely around each of the plumbing pipe vents that go through the roof.

If your finished roof is to be a different material than asphalt shingles, such as cedar shake shingles or metal panels or Spanish tile, you should do some research as to what is involved with installing these types of roofs and the special types of flashings and pipe vent flashings that are required.

Chapter 13

Heating and Air Conditioning

The heating and air conditioning company will begin the next phase of rough-in on the inside of your house. The heating and air conditioning rough-in follows the plumbing because the electrical rough-in should be last. With all the drilling and cutting associated with pipes and ductwork, the wiring should be last to be installed in order to minimize accidental severing of electrical wires.

The heating and air conditioning mechanics will begin installing your forced air system by bringing prefabricated ductwork, made at a sheetmetal shop, to your house. As the mechanics are installing the ductwork for your house's system, they will also be cutting rectangular holes in the plywood floor. These holes are the vents through which the air flows out into the room. If you have a two story house design, the vents upstairs will be in the ceiling, because the air handling systems for the second floor will be located in the attic. Be sure to meet with the heating and air conditioning mechanics to decide upon the location of the vents in each room.

It is a good idea to center vents under windows so that if you have long curtains, the air flow will not be restricted. The mechanics will return to finish the installation of the heating and cooling units toward the end of your construction project.

I elaborated some on the different types of heating and cooling systems back in Chapter 2: House Plans and Design. It is very important to meet with the people at the Energy Resources Department of the utilities company that you are served by. They are qualified to help determine the right system for your house, considering the area in which you live. There are several types of systems available that you may decide on. The hot water baseboard and electric strip baseboard are two of the simplest and easiest systems to install. I wouldn't recommend the electric baseboard unless you are generating your own electricity or have a small area to heat.

The old style water radiator system which uses a boiler and steam pipelines to the radiator is still available and is a good system. Heat generated from steam doesn't usually require any type of fan as it moves by the physics laws of convection and radiation. This type of heat is very beneficial for people who are sensitive to dust which is carried about in a forced air system.

Several years ago there was a lot of emphasis placed on solar heat. There are two types of solar heating systems. The least expensive to install is called passive solar. The design of your house can incorporate a passive solar heating system by simply putting most of the windows for your house on the south side and no windows on the north side. In order for your house to be comfortable in the summer with this type of system, the windows should be the right type, and it helps to have some large deciduous trees on the south side to provide shade.

The active solar system is much more complicated and expensive. It utilizes solar collection panels in which a network of water line pipes allow the heated water to flow through. As the water passes through the collector, it is heated to approximately 150 degrees F. After it leaves the collectors, it passes through another network of water lines that are installed in the floors, walls and ceilings of the house, depending upon the design of the system. If you are planning to use an active solar heating system, do a lot of research and seek the assistance of a professional who has experience with that type of system.

The most popular types of heating and cooling systems today are the forced air types. There are several varieties and combinations available. They all have different capacities and percentages of efficiency.

The older forced air systems utilize a heating furnace that is fueled by either heating oil, kerosene, liquid propane gas or natural gas. For cooling, the system will have a separate unit that has a large compressor fueled with refrigerant. Both furnace and cooling units will be connected to the same duct system that runs throughout the house. As the air is being heated or cooled, it is forced throughout the ductwork system by fans that push the air through the vents in the floor or ceiling and fans that pull air from the rooms through large return vents. The older fuel forced air systems have been improved over the years and have been making a comeback due to people not being satisfied with the newer air heat pump systems.

The newer types of forced air systems are the high efficiency air source and water source heat pumps. The air source heat pump system has built-in heat strips for heating air and refrigerant compressor for cooling air within the same unit. The heat pump unit is installed outside, usually in the back of the house on a concrete pad. This type of heating system has large, heavy duty heatstrip coils, usually 10 k.v., that heat up the air as it is pulled from outside and pumps the warm air through the duct system by fans. It works the same way for cooling, except the heat strips are off and the compressor is on and cooling the outside air as it is pulled through the system. The air source heat pump systems have high efficiency as long as the outside temperature is moderate and not extremely hot or cold. It takes a lot of electricity for a heat pump with a 10 k.v. heat strip to maintain an inside temperature of 78 degrees when it's 20 degrees on the outside. An air heat pump under those conditions will run approximately 40 to 50 minutes of each hour.

The newest of the forced air type systems is the water source heat pump. This system uses the same duct network as the air source system. The main difference in the two systems is that the water source system extracts temperature from water instead of air and then compensates it just as the air source system does. The water source is more efficient because it uses a source for extraction that is consistently the same year round: water. Water that is pulled from at least 10 feet from below the surface is approximately 58 degrees consistently year round. It is not affected by the cold of winter or the heat of summer as the outside air is.

In the compensation process, the water source heat pump uses smaller heat strips, usually 5 k.v. These smaller strips consume a lot less electricity and are used less due to the fact that a substantial amount of heat temperature is transferred from the water. The same principle applies to cooling. The freon compressor is used less because the 58 degree water circulating through the coils provides a lot of cooling to the air that is circulating through the duct system. A minimum amount of compensation is needed to make the temperature in the house what is desired. For the sake of comparison, let's use the same conditions that I stated earlier with the air source heat pump system. If it's 20 degrees outside and you desire the temperature inside to be 78 degrees, the water source system will run approximately 30 to 40 minutes of each hour. This makes a big difference in the amount of electricity consumed because of the smaller heat strips and less time that they are used. I have found that the air blowing out of the vents is warmer with the water source system than the air source system.

The only practical way to have a water source heat pump system is to have a **well** and a place for the discharged water to go. The discharged water is not changed in any way as it is pumped through the pipes and coils of the system and is emptied either into a ditch, pond or back into the well from which it came. It is not cost effective to buy water for this type of system. The cost of a well will make this system more expensive up front, but in the long run the system will pay for itself in saving on the utility bills. I can testify to the efficiency of this system because of the experience we have had in our house. Our house has 2,370 square feet that is heated and cooled. For the past 18 months, our utility bill, which is only electricity, has averaged approximately $115 per month. One factor of this bill is that we have a gas water heater which saves on electricity usage.

The main drawback of this type of system is that you almost always have to have your house on a lot in the country where it is feasible to put a well and have drainage arranged for the discharged water. Be sure to research this type of system thoroughly with the Energy Resource Department at your utility company and with companies that install wells. I highly recommend this system if it fits your application. Ours works great.

If you are not able to have a water source heat pump system for whatever reason, and your climate requires heating and cooling, I recommend a gas pack heating unit and an air conditioning unit that can both use the same duct system. This system is efficient and cost effective.

The gas pack units are designed to use either natural gas that is available in your area or liquid propane (L.P. gas that is stored in a tank on your property and is refilled as needed).

The last type of heat for the home that I will describe is using wood as a source of heat. I used wood as our main source of heat for 11 winters. My wife and I have rented old houses in the country that didn't have any type of conventional heating or cooling systems. The rent would be a lot less than for a comparable house in town. It was my responsibility to provide the heating and cooling for the house. I used a variety of wood heaters over the course of 11 years. I found the Grandpa Fisher® to be the best all around for producing the most heat and for keeping heat generation longer during the hours of the night. A person can save a lot of money on their overall heating costs if they cut and split the wood they use themselves. Using wood as a main source of heat can be very expensive if you have to buy the wood that you use.

The main problem with wood heat is that banks will not qualify a **loan** if a house plan doesn't have a conventional type of heating or cooling system or both, depending on your climate. Using a wood heater requires a lot of work, not only in keeping split wood on hand, but in the process of banking the heater to ensure that it produces enough heat for your house throughout the cold nights. A wood heater must be cleaned out periodically. This can be messy. Our experience with using a wood heater day after day was that fine ash dust accumulated on everything in the house; walls, windows, furniture and especially the TV screen. I feel the greatest health hazard of heating with wood all through the winter is breathing the fine ash dust the heater produces. It increases the occurrence of sore throats, especially with children.

The one good thing about wood heat is that when you come in out of the cold, it's very comforting to back up to a wood heater. The heat radiates and warms you up quickly.

You can certainly use wood as a back-up source of heat if your house plans include a fireplace and chimney. There is something about being warmed by wood burning in the winter that creates a feeling of satisfaction, warmth and togetherness.

I wanted to elaborate on the options that are available for heating and cooling your house because of the importance of making the right choice. The heating and cooling systems are the most expensive of the mechanical systems.

Chapter 14

Electrical

The **electricians** will begin their work on the house in the very beginning after the site preparation. Like the plumbing, the electrical system is installed in three stages. The first thing they do after they receive the **permit** for the house, is to set a service pole in the yard near the house. This pole will have a temporary meter and service receptacles into which several extension cords can be plugged. If it is not code in your area, be sure to have the electrician install at least one receptacle for a 220 volt line. At the time the temporary service is hooked up, the plumbers should have their permit and a spigot stubbed up from the water service. If they haven't, they should be coming to do so soon at that point in time.

The rough-in is the second phase for the electricians. The rough-in for the electricians is similar to that of the plumbers. See the electrical rough-in illustration on the next page. They will drill holes throughout the floors, ceilings and studded walls so that they can pull wires. The wires connect the many switches, receptacles, light fixtures, appliances and the heating and cooling system. They will mount the receptacle, switch and light fixture boxes to the wall studs. All the electrical lines are pulled back to the service breaker box.

You can save approximately $150 on the total electrical quote if your design has an exterior wall on the back of the house that the service box can be mounted on. The code will probably vary from state to state. If the service box can be placed within six feet of the back corner, unless it's too unsightly, it will enable the hook-up of the electrical meter to be installed on the back side of the service box, straight through the wall.

Service panel boxes come in different sizes. For a small house a 100 amp. service is adequate. Most houses that are built today have at least a 150 amp. service which is sufficient for the average size house which will go up to approximately 3,000 square feet. Large houses require at least a 200 amp. service and the really large houses will have two or more service boxes. If you plan to live in your house for a long time, and intend to build outbuildings on your property, have the electrician install a

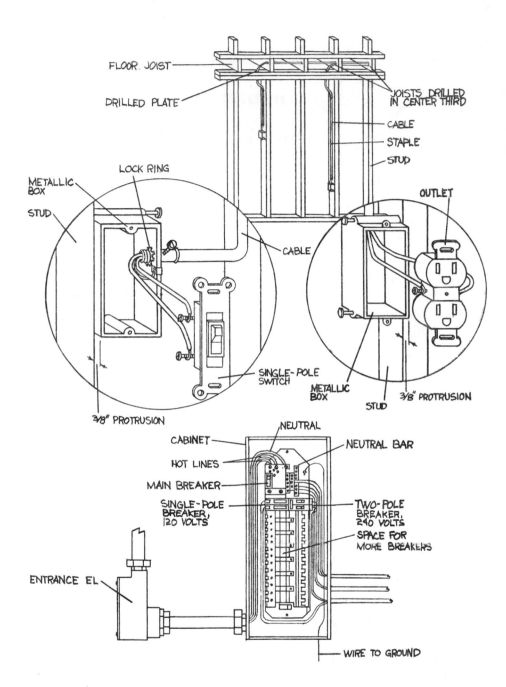

FLOOR JOIST

DRILLED PLATE

JOISTS DRILLED IN CENTER THIRD

CABLE

STAPLE

STUD

LOCK RING

METALLIC BOX

STUD

OUTLET

CABLE

SINGLE-POLE SWITCH

METALLIC BOX

STUD

3/8" PROTRUSION

3/8" PROTRUSION

NEUTRAL

CABINET

NEUTRAL BAR

HOT LINES

MAIN BREAKER

SINGLE-POLE BREAKER, 120 VOLTS

TWO-POLE BREAKER, 240 VOLTS

SPACE FOR MORE BREAKERS

ENTRANCE EL

WIRE TO GROUND

Electrical Rough-in

greater capacity service box for future expansion. I can't stress to you enough the importance of putting a lot of thought into your house project, especially if you anticipate living at your place for many years.

The main areas to check after the electrical rough-in are: that light switches should be 48 inches from the floor and outlets should be 12 inches from the floor; that there is no base wire showing at connections and that all splices are insulated with wire nuts or other plastic connectors; that holes drilled through joists for cables should be near center; outlet and switch boxes should be mounted so that they will be flush with the sheetrock; and that electrical wire be stapled to wall studs within 8 inches of outlet and switch boxes, and at 4-foot intervals. It is very important to take your plans and thoroughly go from room to room to make sure that all the switches, receptacles, ceiling light boxes and appliances lines are all in the correct places. It is much easier to move a receptacle box at this rough-in stage than after the sheetrock is nailed up. Once the rough-in stage is complete, the electricians will not be back until the last few weeks of the project to install the fixtures, box covers and to hook up appliances.

It is very important to make sure that the electricians have nailed a piece of 2 by 4 or 2 by 6 between the ceiling joists, at the place where any ceiling fans are to be mounted. Ceiling fans are heavy and the vibration of the rotating blades will necessitate a very secure mount.

Most electrical contractors will include pulling telephone cable and mounting wall jacks in their quoted price. Be sure to check this out in the early negotiating stages when you are getting quotes. If the electricians are wiring your house for phones, go from room to room with them and be sure you have indicated everywhere you think you could possibly want to have a phone jack. The cost up front of pulling cable and mounting wall jacks at this stage is very minimal compared to what it would cost after your house is finished.

I would like to recommend to you something that I did that I believe is a good idea. If you know where you are going to put your stereo system, have the electricians run speaker wire from the stereo location through the walls to where the speakers will be. In our living room, there is only one place that the stereo could be placed, so it was an easy decision as to where the wires could be pulled for the speakers to be plugged in.

Some other wiring suggestions I would like to offer is that you have wall switch controls for your ceiling fans and also for table lamps. It's a nice convenience to walk into a room at night and flip a wall switch that turns on table lamps on the other end of the room. You may want to consider dimmer wall switches for some of your overhead ceiling lights. If you choose speed control switches for the ceiling fan and you have young children, it's a good idea to have the switches mounted about a foot above the standard height for wall switches. We had this done in our house. We don't find the switches to be unattractive at all and at the height of 5 feet, it keeps the little ones from bothering with switches they shouldn't bother with.

The electricians will return to your project within the last two or three weeks before you close out the construction loan and have the final inspection. Your house should be basically finished except for touch-ups. The electricians should be very careful as they are installing the fixtures you have previously selected. It's important that they do things like put down an old blanket or piece of carpet to slide appliances across the new floor in the kitchen to prevent possible damage. Sometimes the spaces in the cabinets are not quite large enough for the dishwasher, stove or refrigerator. It's best to call the cabinet installer to adjust the cabinets rather than to allow the electricians to possibly do some damage by trying to force the appliances.

You are your own best inspector. Check the mounting of the ceiling fans to make sure the electricians have put large enough screws into the ceiling joists to hold the fan securely. All receptacle and switch covers should be flush on the wall surface and perpendicular. The base of ceiling light fixtures should be flush on the ceiling.

As the electricians are finishing the inside, they will have the current circuit system and main cables ready to mount an electrical meter to the outside of your house. The utilities company will install the meter once the final **inspection** has been completed and you are about to move into your house. You may want to consider having an underground service cable installed instead of the standard overhead cable that requires a utility pole. If you are building in a subdivision, most likely you will have underground service anyway. Requesting underground for a lot in the country will cost approximately $250 extra if your house is not more than 200 feet from the road and overhead service. If you are building farther from the road than 200 feet, the utilities company will figure the cost of installing overhead lines to your house and the cost for underground cable to your house. Underground is considerably more expensive. After the engineers have figured the cost both ways, your charge for going with underground will be the difference of the cost of the overhead subtracted from the cost of the underground. We chose to have underground installed. It cost $998 to install the underground from the highway to the house meter which is 1,580 feet. That's a rather large extra expense, but we simply didn't want to see large utility poles with overhead lines strung across the landscape.

This completes the description of the mechanical stages of work. After all three mechanical rough-ins have been completed and the inspections have been approved, the house shell is ready for insulation. Before I cover the information on house insulation, I wanted to include some other types of work that can be taking place on the outside of the house while the mechanical rough-ins are happening on the inside of the house.

The company you have selected and scheduled to put the exterior veneer on your house can begin after the electrical rough-in is finished. These people will need to meet with the framers, or whoever is doing the boxing for your house, in order to determine what will have to be done so that the boxing and exterior veneer will finish out properly. The exterior veneer can be brick, stone, wood, vinyl siding, exterior plywood, wood shingles, wood shakes, paneling, aluminum siding, masonite siding, or logs. If you are building a log house, the logs will be the frame for the walls, the exterior finish and possibly the interior finish if that is the look that you choose.

During the mechanical rough-ins is also an ideal time to have the **septic tank** company come and install the tank and drainage lines, if your house requires a septic tank. The septic tank installer will have to have a copy of the Health Department's permit. This will enable the equipment operators to measure and place the tank and lines in the places that the Health Department engineers have designated. It's a good idea to be at your lot when they start to make sure that they are following the instructions that are on the permit. Ask the backhoe operator to backfill and grade the area where the tank and lines are. This will help the **landscaper** and will possibly lower his price.

I wanted to interject these exterior types of work that could be going on during the mechanical rough-in stage because you need to make every good weather day count. It's very frustrating to be finishing up your house and want to close the construction and mortgage loans and you can't because the monsoons have set in and it's too wet to have the septic system put in and the finishing landscaping done. Keep your construction project progressing along on the inside and outside by scheduling the right people at the right times.

Chapter 15

Insulation

Building an energy efficient house begins with your design, as I expressed in Chapter 2 relating to Design and House Plans. Energy efficiency is affected by the care taken in the construction of each stage of the project. For example, the foundation or masonry contractor should insulate the foundation properly if your house has a basement or if you live in an extremely cold climate; the framers should frame the shell square and plumb so that insulation bats, exterior windows and doors fit tightly; caulking should be applied around the base plate of the subfloors and any cracks that will allow air to penetrate into the house; the mechanical contractors should plug and seal any openings that were made when they installed the pipes, ductwork and wires; the insulators should install the batts, blown insulation and vapor barrier properly to ensure thorough coverage; the drywall hangers should be careful not to damage the vapor barrier as they are hanging the sheetrock.

The general contractor is responsible for supervising the workmanship of the construction project. This is your house that you look forward to living in. Make sure the craftspeople that are building it build it right and energy efficient.

I would like to reiterate the importance of spending time with the Energy Resources Department of your local utilities commission company. The people who work in that department can give you many suggestions on how to build your house with greater energy efficiency. It would be very disappointing to build a simply gorgeous house with lots of amenities, but one that runs up a utility bill averaging $300 per month.

Insulation and other building materials such as exterior sheathing are given a rating known as an **R-value**. The R-value is a measure of the capacity of a material to impede or resist heat flow through it. The greater the R-value number, the greater the capacity of the material to lessen the transfer of heat through its composition.

There are several types of insulation. I will list the types with a brief description of each. Batts are fiberglass or rock wool insulation that have paper facings and are precut to fit tightly between wall studs, floor joists and ceiling rafters. This is the most common type of insulation due to its low cost, ease of installation and its fire safety properties. The **R-value** for batts is 3.2 per inch. Some disadvantages are that moisture and compression reduces the R-value. The fibers are also very irritating to the skin and anyone installing batts should be completely clothed and use a dust mask.

Loose fill insulation is made of several materials, of which cellulose, fiberglass and rock wool are the most common. This type is blown or poured into the attic floor or walls. This insulation, like batts, is inexpensive, has good fire safety properties and is easy to install if it is poured from the bags. If it is blown, it requires special equipment and is usually done by an insulation company. The R-value for the cellulose and rock wool are the same per inch as batts. The R-value for loose fill fiberglass insulation is less: 2.2 per inch. This type of insulation has the same disadvantages as batts.

Rigid board insulation has become very popular as the exterior sheathing that goes on before the siding or brick veneer and the interior sheathing that goes on before sheetrock. It is made from a variety of materials, such as expanded and extruded polystyrene, urethane, isocyanurate, phenolic foam and rigid fiberglass. Besides being widely used for interior and exterior wall sheathing, this type of insulation is also used for foundations, basement walls, attic roofs, masonry walls and floors over unheated spaces. Rigid board insulation has high R-values ranging from 5 per inch for the extruded polystyrene type, to 7.2 per inch for urethane, to 8.2 per inch for phenolic foam. Some of the disadvantages of rigid board insulation are its high cost and its deterioration in sunlight. Also, some types are flammable and some contain fluorocarbons which degrade the ozone.

Foam-in-place insulation is a fairly new type of insulation that is excellent for remodeling an old house that does not have any insulation or very little wall insulation. This type is urethane foam and is foamed into the walls and roof cavities through small holes. Along with having a high R-value of 6.2 per inch, it does a thorough job of filling in around wires, pipes and crevices. The disadvantages of it are its high cost for professional installation, it is combustible, and has fluorocarbons.

Spray-in-place insulation has the same installation concept as foam-in-place insulation. Spray-in-place is cellulose with binder that is sprayed into walls and roof cavities through small holes. It fills in around wires, etc., as the urethane does but has a lower R-value of 3.2 per inch. It is not combustible nor does it have fluorocarbons, but it is vulnerable to moisture.

The types of insulation and amounts of the types required for your house will vary from one climate region to another. For example, the recommended **R-values** for a house built in southern Florida or southern Texas are R-19 for ceilings, R-12 for walls, R-11 for roofs and R-2 for windows. The recommended R-value for houses built in the states of the far north are R-49 for ceilings, R-22 for walls, R-25 for roofs and R-4 or 5 for windows. The right combinations of materials and quantities of materials to provide the desirable R-value for your house can be established by the professionals at your local utilities or insulation company. Ask them to explain the **E-300** program to you (see illustration on following page).

Properly insulating your house is important, but equally important is protecting your house from the infiltration of **moisture.** Moisture greatly reduces the R-value of insulation materials and, more importantly, it causes wood to rot over a period of time. There are two forms of moisture that can damage your house. The liquid water form can penetrate your house through holes in the roof or siding when it rains, or can erupt from a water line leak in the plumbing system. Recognizing these types of moisture problems should be obvious and in a new home should not happen due to proper construction and inspections.

The type of moisture that is much more difficult to detect and eliminate is water vapor which is in a gas form. This vapor is not really a problem until it condensates and changes from vapor to liquid. In the winter, the warmer air inside your house holds a lot more water than the cold air outside of your house. If the warm air with the water vapor is able to penetrate through the sheetrock and insulation, it will begin to cool as it nears the exterior walls of your house. The cooler temperature penetrating from the outside wall will cause the vapor to condensate into liquid which will then collect in the insulation and on the wall studs of the perimeter walls, floor joists and roof rafters. Water vapor defuses easily through drywall.

There are several ways to prevent water vapor problems. After the foundation walls and piers are layed, take a root rake and hand grade the sand that is inside your house foundation. Next roll out a heavy mill polyethylene plastic over the ground. Cut the lengths and shovel some sand on the ends to help keep it in place. This **vapor barrier** will prevent a lot of moisture from rising up from the sand under your house, and the mechanical subcontractor workers who will be crawling under your house will appreciate it, too. It's much easier to put it down before the framers start than after the house is framed and built.

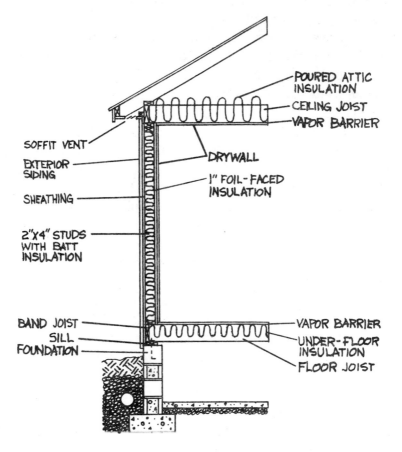

POURED ATTIC INSULATION

CEILING JOIST

VAPOR BARRIER

SOFFIT VENT

EXTERIOR SIDING

SHEATHING

2"x4" STUDS WITH BATT INSULATION

DRYWALL

1" FOIL-FACED INSULATION

BAND JOIST

SILL

FOUNDATION

VAPOR BARRIER

UNDER-FLOOR INSULATION

FLOOR JOIST

Wall Cross Section

Check out the new house wraps that are available for wrapping your house once it's framed. The house wrap is rolled over and nailed to the walls after the sheathing is put up. This house wrap prevents air from penetrating through the joints of the sheathing and makes a tight fit around the doors and windows. The putting on of a house wrap is optional. On the inside of your house, a **vapor barrier** should be put down on top of the floor joists before the subfloor is put down. This will prevent vapor from penetrating through the insulation that will be between the floor joists. In some areas, the vapor barrier is put between the subfloor and the floor and instead of using polyethylene, roofing paper is used. For the interior walls, a water vapor barrier of usually 6 mil polyethylene is stapled to the wall studs after the insulation batts are put into place. This procedure is now code in most, if not all, of America. A vapor barrier should also be stapled to the ceilings prior to the sheetrock being hung.

If your house has a heated attic, there should be one inch foil faced rigid board insulation put up before the drywall. It's very important that the insulation batts that are between the roof rafters not be too thick. If the rafters are 2-inch by 10-inch, the batts should be eight inches thick or less in order to allow for an air space for ventilation. This space is called a baffle and is an important part of the soffit and ridge vent system for ventilation. There must be air flow between the insulation and the roof sheathing in order to prevent ice accumulation in the winter and to keep the roof surface cooler in the summer heat.

To summarize building an energy efficient house: have the energy services people at your utilities company do an **E-300** workup from your house plans; put a vapor barrier down on the sand under your house; have vapor barriers installed on the warm (interior) side of walls, ceilings and floors; insulators should be careful not to compress the batts that they are installing; framers and mechanical workers should caulk and seal all of the air leaks; specify low-e or gas filled double pane windows such as Anderson® windows for your house; specify insulated metal doors for the exterior of your house; insulation in the roof must not touch the sheathing; and the attic must have soffit and ridge vents for ventilation. It's also a good idea to have a thermostatically controlled fan ventilation in the attic to push hot air out in the heat of summer.

Some of these precautionary measures cost more up front, but will certainly make a savings difference on your utility bill in the long run.

Chapter 16

Interior Wall Finishing

The mechanical rough-ins have been inspected and approved, and the insulation and vapor barriers have been installed, which means the next work to be done is the interior wall finishing. This is the work that makes your house come together and begin to have a finished look.

There are several types of wall finishes available, such as gypsum board, plaster and paneling. The most common by far is **gypsum board**. Other names for it are **drywall** and **sheetrock**. Drywall sheets are smooth finished on the front side and cardboard rough on the back side. These sheets are four feet wide and either 10, 12 or 16 feet in length. There are two common thicknesses for residential building. The one-half inch thick sheets are used for walls throughout all rooms and closets. The 5/8 inch thick sheets are heavier and are used for the ceilings. On some house plans, some walls will call for 5/8 inch wall board to help with soundproofing. There are basically three types of gypsum board: the standard, which is relatively fire resistant, accommodates most applications; the fireproof, which is required by code in some areas; and the water resistant drywall, which is also called green board because of its green paper. It is used in bathrooms and other areas that are exposed to a lot of moisture. All three of these types of drywall, properly hung and finished, will provide smooth wall surfaces that paint, wallpaper, paneling or tile can be applied to.

The drywall hangers will begin by cutting and then nailing or screwing the sheets or panels to the ceiling joists. After all the ceilings are covered, the hangers will begin cutting and nailing or screwing the sheets to cover the walls. The long edges of the sheets are tapered and the short edges are the full thickness of the sheet. In nearly all applications, drywall will be hung with the length of the sheets running horizontal on the walls. The tapered edges should always meet and the untapered edges should always meet. There shouldn't be any mismatching of the edges, due to the difficulty of finishing them. If the hangers leave 1/8 inch cracks between the edges, that's ok and is much preferred over the sheets being tightly fitted together. Joints that are tight together will most likely bulge.

There are special nails and screws made for securing the drywall panels to the ceilings and walls. The nails are grooved and the screws have a wide space between the spirals. Both are designed to hold tightly to the wood studs. The **drywall** nails or screws should be applied approximately every 16 inches on the sheets going into the ceiling joists and wall studs. The nails should be driven or countersunk below the surface of the panels and the screws should be screwed below the flush surface of the panels. This is required in order to facilitate proper finishing. In your area, drywall adhesive may be required to satisfy the building code. The drywall adhesive is a black paste and is smeared onto the wall studs prior to nailing or screwing the panels to the wall.

Throughout your house there will be walls that meet from outside and inside corners. The drywall finishers will nail a strip of metal called corner beads to the outside corners and "J" or "L" beads to the inside corners. This creates a more defined angle on the corners to produce a more professional finish.

The next step for the finishers is mudding and taping the joints, corners and recessed nail or screw heads. The finishers will apply a thin layer of joint compound mud to the joints, corners and fastener heads using various sizes of mud knives. The paper tape is 2 inches wide and carefully placed over the mud and smoothed out with wide mud knives. Joint compound only is used to cover the indented fastener head spots. After the tape has sufficiently dried, two and sometimes three more applications of joint compound are applied. This procedure produces a flat, smooth surface that is ready for the final wall treatment. Once each application is dry, the wall should be sanded smooth.

There are several ways you can finish the ceilings in your house. The quickest and least expensive is to have the ceiling sprayed which produces the rough textured look. Most drywall companies offer the spraying as part of finishing. It usually costs considerably more to have the finishers prepare the ceiling for painting due to the difficulty of working overhead.

Ceiling tile is another option that offers many different styles and textures, but costs a lot more than spraying or painting the ceiling. To install ceiling tile, thin narrow boards are nailed or screwed perpendicularly across the ceiling joists. The correct width apart will allow the edges of the tiles to meet over the boards with enough space on either side for fastening. The tiles are then interlocked and stapled or tacked on the inside edge. Some of the newer styles have metal track that is mounted to the ceiling and the tiles are then simply dropped into place. Ceiling tiles are very decorative and can really change the look of a room.

If your heart is set on having the inside of your house finished with **plaster walls,** there are still some companies that can do the job. Cost is certainly a factor. Generally having walls finished with plaster costs about twice as much per square foot as sheetrock. That adds up quick. Plaster has its advantages. It produces a more beautiful finish and is more soundproof. Having been raised in a house with plaster walls and ceilings, I personally believe that the plaster walls are cooler in the heat of the summer.

There are two predominate ways to make a plaster wall. The quickest and easiest way is using a type of backboard called gypsum lathe. This board is nailed to the studs similar to hanging sheetrock or drywall. Plaster is then applied with large trowels in two different applications. Each application is approximately one-fourth inch thick.

The old style approach was used before the production of the gypsum lathe board. The plasterers would cut and fit a metal lathe, which is approximately one-half inch square mesh and nail it to the wall studs. The same technique is used as when plastering a gypsum lathe, but instead of two applications there are three, and the applications are thicker. Plaster will enhance the wall beauty of any home.

Chapter 17

Finished Flooring

Finish carpenters specialize in one, some, or all of the types of precision woodwork that completes the finished look of the inside of a house. Finding one company or individual that can do it all is rare, but if you are fortunate enough to do so, you will probably be able to save a lot of money. I wasn't able to find the one crew that could do it all. We ended up with four different subcontractors due to conflicting schedules and some specialty cabinet work. I was and still am very pleased with the quality of woodwork performed in our house.

When selecting the finish carpenters that are going to do the precision woodwork for the interior of your house, be sure you ask to see some of their work. Finish or trim carpenters' work begins when the finishing of the walls is complete. The crew will begin by setting up all of their saws and equipment. They will begin working on the floors first. They will cut, fit and nail down the underlayment for hardwood floor boards.

The underlayment is sheets of either plywood, fiberboard or particle board. I highly recommend one-half inch heel proof plywood if you are planning to live in your house several years. Before the carpenters begin to measure and cut the underlayment, they should thoroughly sweep each room and then roll out and cover each subfloor with roofing felt paper. The felt paper serves as a moisture barrier and gives a little insulation. The carpenters will cut and fit the sheets of underlayment so that each joint is tight. They will then nail the underlayment down to the subfloor. This is also the time for them to cut out the vents for the heating and air conditioning vent work in the floor system. Once the underlayment is down, the floor is ready for the finish covering of either hardwood slats, vinyl, carpet or ceramic or wood tile.

Hardwood floors are more expensive to have put down than the other types of coverings, but they really add a warm look to a room. Unless specially ordered, hardwood slats for floors will either be red oak, maple or pine. The slats are interlocking tongue and grooved and are available in different widths, lengths and grades. The top grade will be clear grain with the least number of knots.

The slats come from the saw mills in bundles which contain several shades of the wood's color. A good hardwood floor carpenter will pick through the pile so that the light and dark shades are intermingled as he is nailing the floor down. This eliminates having areas in the finished floor that are too heavy with either light or dark shades of the wood's color.

The tongue and grooved slats are nailed to the subfloor with old style cut nails. This same process and type of nails was popular 50 years ago.

A newly laid hardwood floor requires a lot of finish work to make it look good. I have included in Chapter 21, Hardwood Floor Finishing, information about how to do a good finish job on hardwood floors.

There are two types of vinyl flooring and two forms that are available. Inlaid and non-inlaid are the two types and they are available in either tiles or rolled sheets. There are many designs and quality grades of vinyl to choose from. Top grade inlaid vinyl can be expensive, especially for some of the designer type patterns. Inlaid means that the colors on the surface of the vinyl go all the way through the sheets or tiles. This type of flooring is more durable and will look better a lot longer than the non-inlaid. The non-inlaid vinyl has the color baked on a dark vinyl base as a veneer. After wear, dents and scratches, the dark base begins to show through. Non-inlaid is a good grade for pantries, or closets but not for high traffic areas that are most noticeable in rooms such as the kitchen.

Vinyl is available in either 9 x 9 inch or 12 x 12 inch sheets and rolled sheets that are made up to 12 feet in width. This width size works great for 12-foot wide rooms and smaller because there are not any seams. This is something you may want to consider if you are designing your own plans. The tiles and the sheets can be put down over plywood underlayment or a concrete slab using a special thin set adhesive. If you are using concrete slab floors, I suggest a plywood floor underlayment to eliminate moisture problems and to make the vinyl covered floor warmer.

Ceramic tile flooring for a long time was seen primarily in bathrooms and patios or porches, but is gaining popularity as a desirable floor covering for kitchens and foyers. Also ceramic tiles are increasingly being used as wall covering for sections of kitchens and for kitchen counter tops.

The installation of ceramic tile is a specialty that is generally performed by an experienced mason. The tile can be laid over concrete slab floors or plywood underlayment if it is at least five-eighths inch thick. The thicker, heavier plywood is used to prevent flexing, because the tile and grouted joints will crack if the subfloor gives any.

The mason performing the tile work will use one of three methods. The oldest method is called "mud set" in which the mason lays the tile over a bed of 1-inch thick mortar. The joints are then grouted with a special cement mix.

The most common method used today is the thin set method. This method is much quicker to install because the special cement, sand and latex bonding mix are spread on about one-fourth inch thick and dries much faster. The joints are then grouted as with the mud set method.

A third method of installing ceramic tile is using mastic adhesive. This is used for special applications such as kitchen walls and countertops. Ceramic tile adds a different and distinctive look to the inside of a home. Again, it is all up to the individuals building the house as to the look and type of materials used for the finishings.

Carpet is by far the largest square footage floor covering used in houses today. Hardwood floors, vinyl and ceramic tile should be put down after the floor underlayment and before cabinets and finish carpentry begins, but carpet should be the last thing that is installed in your new home. The reason for this is because carpet can be installed in each room up to the already nailed up base or floor molding. The other floor coverings should be put down before the base molding is nailed on.

Carpet, like vinyl, comes in a large variety of colors, grades, materials, textures and styles. Finding the right carpet at the price for your house is a real challenge. I believe my wife and I spent more time looking and deciding on carpet than we did on all the other interior cosmetics combined. ("Interior cosmetics" is my terminology for what is actually seen in the interior of a finished house such as the floor coverings, painted or stained wood trims and cabinets, and painted, papered or tiled walls.)

When you begin looking at carpet, remember that you get a better deal if you can decide on one color and style for the whole house. If you have children, I highly recommend any of the new types of carpet that have the stain resistant finishes. They clean up so well with shampooing that it's like having new carpet all over again. These types are more expensive but certainly look better a lot longer than the varieties that don't have the stain resistant finishes.

The carpet installers will begin by nailing down thin, narrow strips of wood along the perimeter walls of each room, next to the floor molding. These strips of wood have short, pointed barbs sticking up that hold the nap of the underside of the carpet once it is stretched and fitted. Before the installers fit and stretch the carpet, they will roll out and fit the padding.

Padding, like carpet, comes in a variety of types and grades. We found that a good quality waffle foam rubber type padding is most recom-mended for carpet that is being put down in high traffic areas such as hallways, stairs and living rooms. This type of padding is more expen-sive than the cushion foam rubber type padding, but will not deteriorate and break up nearly as quickly. The cushion foam rubber type is about half as expensive as the waffle type, but simply will not hold up as long in high traffic areas. We saved some money by having the cushion foam type padding put in our bedrooms. The other advantage for foam type is that it is noticeably softer to walk on, especially under bare feet, than the waffle type.

Chapter 18

Interior Doors and Trim Moldings

After the floor underlayment is down, the finish carpenters can begin work on trim moldings, hanging interior doors, putting the casing around the doors and windows, staircases, cabinets, mantles and vanities. Depending on the size of the crew, all of this could be going on at one time or just one type of work going on at a time. I will cover each area of this finish carpentry work and give you a few tips along the way.

Interior doors come in a variety of types, styles and dimensions, and vary a lot in price. One thing that will be a factor in the finish carpentry price is whether you choose pre-hung doors or not. Pre-hung doors can be installed a lot quicker than those that aren't pre-hung. Pre-hung means the doors have all the casing and trim already precut and nailed together around the doors, and have been mortised. Mortising is the drilling of holes in the doors where the knobs and works go and the cutting of slots where the flush fitting hinges go. This process takes a considerable amount of time. The pre-hung door is more expensive than the nonpre-hung door but can save significantly on trim materials and the carpenter's time and price.

I chose this type of door and I suggest that you price it with your building supply salesman. The pre-hung door looks just as nice as those that have to have all of the different types of work done to them.

The amount of money that you spend on interior doors will be determined by the quality and the finished look that you want. I don't recommend that you use the less expensive, plain, hollow doors in entrances to the rooms in your house. These type doors may suffice on closets in order to help save some money, but for room entrance doors, the solid wood doors that have panels on either side give more of a quality look to your house. Also available are masonite doors which can be ordered pre-hung with decorative panels. They are a little more expensive than the hollow doors, but they certainly look better. Their only drawback is that they cannot be stained, only painted.

The finish carpenters should meticulously shim, level and nail solid each door using large finish nails. Each door should be adjusted to make sure the door swings freely and latches securely.

The windows of your house are to be cased and trimmed using a variety of types of milled lumber. The top, sides and bottom of the windows are framed with casing or trim. It is available in $2^1/2$ inch, $3^1/4$ inch and $4^1/4$ inch sizes and comes in different styles.

The flat shelf-like trim that is at the bottom of the window, above the bottom trim, is called the "stool". This piece requires close cuts and tight fits to ensure a good finish. All of these types of trim enhance the beauty of windows when they are properly fitted and finished.

There are several things to consider when selecting the types of moldings, trim and materials for cabinets and vanities. The main decision to arrive at is what in your house in the way of trim and cabinets is going to be stained and what is going to be painted. You can certainly save a lot of money by painting everything. But if you're like me, you like the warm, rich look of stained wood when it's a smooth, deep grain. If you are not into stained wood, the type of trim for the windows and doors and the base, chair rail and crown moldings should be what is called finger jointed molding. This type of trim and molding is made of short pieces of wood fitted and glued together, and then run through the mill to produce its finished look. This type of trim of molding is a lot less expensive than the No. 2 or better, clear white pine or white oak, which is commonly used for staining. Once the finger jointed wood is painted, it looks just as good as top grade molding or trim that costs four times as much.

Sometimes the architect or **draftsperson** who has drawn your set of plans will include a detailed molding plan for each room. If your set of plans does not have a molding detail or if your plans do and you want to save money by not using it, I have suggested a simple molding plan that will help you save some bucks.

The least number of times a trim carpenter has to go around a room putting up molding, the less his price will be for the job, because time is money. By specifying one piece base molding, one piece chair rail molding, and one piece crown molding for your rooms, you keep the carpenter's number of trips around the room to three. One piece means that the molding is milled so that it looks like two or more pieces nailed together but really isn't. If you decided on base molding with a cap, two piece chair rail, and two piece crown with additional dental mold, you would be paying the trim carpenter to go around the room seven times and paying for all the extra moldings. The one piece moldings are available in either the finger joint or clear grain. When you compare the one piece moldings with the two or more piece arrangements, you'll be amazed at how close they look alike and the difference in the pricing, especially when you add the carpenter's labor for the extra trips.

The finish carpenters cut the measured moldings and trims on a miter saw. This saw allows the carpenters to cut precise angles and bevels. Often a carpenter will have to use a small, thin blade hand saw to trim and cut to make a tight fit at the joints. Once each piece is properly cut and fitted together, it is nailed up in place tight with finishing nails. The molding joints should not have any cracks or gaps wider than 1/32 inch. Another checkpoint to inspect during the installation of the moldings and door and window trims is to make sure that each room has the correct moldings for that room.

The wooden doors, trim for the doors and all the moldings should be sanded and ready for either paint or stain, unless you are doing the painting or staining and have already taken care of that prior to the installation of the wood. More on that in Chapter 22, Staining Cabinetry and Trim Moldings.

The carpenter should take nail sets and sink each finishing nail about one-eighth inch below the surface of the wood. This is so that wood putty can be applied to cover the nail heads prior to painting and staining.

Something that is important for the carpenters to do who are putting up the moldings that are to be stained is to pick through the moldings in order to match as closely as possible similar grained pieces. The shade of stained wood will vary a lot depending on what part of the tree the piece of molding was cut from. A piece of molding cut from the heart of a white pine will stain lighter with a red tint compared to a piece cut from the outer layers of the tree, which is softer wood. It will stain much darker. The soft wood is more porous and will soak up more stain unless the wood is properly prepared for staining.

Chapter 19

Cabinetry and Counter Tops

There is a lot of information available on cabinetry. Many books have been written on this subject which requires a lot of experience to produce quality work. Cabinetry work includes kitchen cabinets, vanities, home entertainment centers, pantries, bookshelves and desks.

The design and style of your cabinetry is again a personal preference. You may prefer to choose prefabricated cabinets that the building supply house can offer instead of having a cabinet maker custom build a set for you. The type of material used, the design, and style will make the difference in the price of your cabinets. Again, painting is much less expensive than staining cabinetry. You just simply have to weigh the cost factor against the look you really want in order make your decision.

Debbie and I spent several hours researching and studying cabinets for the kitchen and vanities for the bathroom. We looked through many catalogs offering every kind of kitchen cabinet imaginable. But again, it was like our experience looking for the house plan that was right for us. We couldn't find what we wanted in the right combination of wood type, design and door style. Whenever we found something that was close to what we wanted, it was much more expensive than what we could afford.

Quality built cabinets, whether ordered prefabricated or custom built locally, can be very expensive. We found that by having the cabinets custom built locally, we were able to get the cabinets we wanted and were able to afford them.

One thing that we discovered about the prefab cabinets was that almost every manufacturer used particle board covered with wood veneer for the boxes and shelves. When I discovered that, the decision as to what type of cabinets to order was easy for me to make. Particle board has many applications and is about one-half as expensive as plywood. My personal decision was not to use it unless we absolutely could not afford the higher quality plywood. We were very fortunate that we were able to manage the construction loan in a way that allowed us to have the kitchen cabinets that we truly wanted custom built.

When deciding on any type of cabinetry, function should take priority over all other aspects. After all, the practicality of cabinets is that they are used for storage and should have conveniences. The best way to determine the types of features you want in your cabinets is to go to open house walk-throughs that real estate companies offer when marketing new houses. Check out the turntables in the corners of the cabinets, the glass doors and the storage compartments in the pantries. You begin to get a feel for what you want as you inspect the arrangement of the kitchen cabinets and appliances. The kitchen needs to be the most organized room in the house. It's important, especially if you plan to live in your house a long time, to design your kitchen cabinets and appliances so that they are arranged in the most convenient order.

Whether you design your cabinets yourself, or are having someone else design them for you, or are ordering a set through a company, be sure that your cabinet plan or layout does not have any cabinet or appliance doors blocking one another. There should be free access and swing of all doors.

Along with inspecting new homes that are for sale, as you begin looking around you will find a lot of good design information in books and magazines. Also your building supply salesman should have tons of catalogs on prefab cabinets that will have many layouts and features to help you make your decisions.

Cabinets with all their different styles and looks are actually in one of two categories. The traditional face frame is the type that has beauty molding or picture frame molding cut and fitted with rectangles on the fronts of the doors and drawer fronts. A more expensive version of this category is the raised panel doors and drawer fronts. The face frame style of cabinets will have, unless special ordered, spaces between the doors and countertops that are called styles and rails. The style will almost always have door and drawer pulls which are part of the traditional look.

The other category of cabinet styles is called frameless cabinets which offer the contemporary look. The frameless look is smooth with no pulls or framework and the hinges are concealed. Instead of pulls to assist in opening the doors, there are finger grooves recessed in the bottom of the doors, opposite from the hinges and in the middle of the bottom of the door fronts. Frameless cabinets also differ from the face frame style in that they don't have the style and rail spaces showing. The doors are made so that the front or face side of the cabinet box frame is not showing. This is another feature of the contemporary look which is basically smooth.

Cabinets may vary a lot in looks and style but there are some standards that are universal. As a rule the standard height for base cabinets is 33 inches and then 1½ inch for the thickness of the countertop. The countertop should be 24 inches deep (from the front to the wall), unless the cabinet bases have an unusual application. Above the base unit and countertop will be the wall cabinets, which are hung on the wall and sometimes from the ceiling. The wall cabinets are usually 12 inches deep and always vary in width or length depending upon the design layout. An old style for wall cabinet doors that is gaining popularity, is the insertion of clear stained or etched glass. These type of doors add a nice touch to any kitchen.

Your cabinets and vanities, whether prefab or custom built locally, will be delivered to your house and installed in sections. The cabinet makers should be scheduled to deliver and install the cabinets after the sheetrock is finished and the floor underlayment is down. The final floor finishes that should be completed at this stage are hardwood floors and ceramic tile floors. Vinyl covering and any type of carpet that might be selected to go in your kitchen, should be installed after the base units are installed.

The wall cabinet sections will be mounted first. The carpenters should start from the corner of the kitchen and work out. The installation and aligning is tedious with a lot of shimming and leveling in order to set the cabinets plumb and level. The cabinets should be screwed to the pre-located wall studs with fairly large wood screws for stability.

After the top wall cabinets are hung, the large base units are brought in and the installation process begins all over with the carpenters starting from the corner of the room. Some cabinet makers install the drawer glides during the base box building while it's in the shop, others install the glides after the units are mounted into the kitchen. I recommend that whether you are ordering prefabricated units or having your cabinets custom built, your cabinet drawers have glides on either side. They work much better than the less expensive single tract type that is installed under the center of the drawers.

The countertops are brought in after the doors and drawers. Countertops like the cabinet boxes, doors and drawer fronts are available in many types of materials and looks. It's amazing the variety to choose from today in deciding the look that a person wants for each room of their house. Some of the different types of materials and looks available for countertops are formica, which is the most common and is a type of plastic laminate, available in hundreds of colors and patterns; ceramic tile; stone, which is about three-fourths inch thick and there are several brands of synthetic stone that look like laminate; and the butcher block wood type. All of these materials are durable and can be applied on top of quality plywood.

Some cabinet and vanity designs call for a backsplash. This is a relatively old feature, but is still practical. The backsplash can be different sizes but is usually 3½ inches wide by approximately three-fourths inch thick and the length of the countertop. The 3½ inch side fastens flat against the wall and serves as protection for the wall where it joins the countertop. These are most commonly found in the vanities and sometimes around kitchen countertops.

Countertops and cabinets are nearly always sold by the linear or running foot. Good quality cabinets will be in the price range of $60 to $180 per foot. Countertops that are made from plastic formica laminate covered plywood start as low as $20 per foot with the most expensive type being synthetic stone which can be as much as $160 per running foot.

Chapter 20

Mantles and Staircases

Mantles and staircases are another specialized area of finished carpentry. A decorative mantle that expresses the overall style of the interior and exterior of the house will be a real focal point that will greatly enhance the beauty of the room that it is in. Mantles can be as simple as a single heavy hand-hewn board, sanded and stained for a truly rustic effect, to the elaborate Williamsburg style with a face plate, legs on either side and several types of trim moldings for detail. Any experienced trim carpenter or cabinetmaker should be able to build the style of mantle you want from a picture, usually at a price less than the cost and installation of a prefabricated mantle. I believe that by having one custom built, you get a closer fit and a mantle made of better quality materials.

There are several companies that mass produce all styles and sizes of mantles. Some even custom build to your specifications and can make them from a variety of exotic woods for stainings. Your building supply salesman is your best source for catalogs from the mantle making companies. The companies sell direct to the building supply companies, which increases the cost by about 15 to 20 percent. I contracted our cabinetmaker to build our mantle out of solid white oak for about $150, which was a really good price.

It's very important all the way through the whole construction process to decide early on what you want and to compare prices. When you save $100 here or $200 there, before you know it, you have saved $1,000 by being a thrifty shopper.

I never realized how involved staircases are until I began watching the carpenter that I had contracted to help us with ours began to install it. This man had been doing this type of work in his spare time for approximately 20 years and was an expert. It was fascinating to watch him measure and precisely drill holes in the underside of the handrail, or banister, as it's called, for the fitting of the many pickets. Basic, nothing fancy stairrail costs approximately $3 per foot. All of the picket or banister holes have to be exactly centered, placed in the same distance apart and drilled consistently the same depth in order for the rail to fit properly. One hole drilled in error could ruin a very expensive piece of hand rail wood.

There are many parts to a staircase and they are available in styles from simple and basic to very elaborate and expensive. See the staircase illustration on page 134. The staircase installer will start where the framers finished.

Remember the framers? The framers cut and nailed 2-inch by 8-inch boards across the stair carriage. The finish carpenter who is installing the staircase will rip these temporary boards out. He then will measure, cut and nail down the finish stringer boards on either side of the stairway. On top of the stringers, there will be a piece of trim molding called a cap. The finish boards that are the actual steps are called treads. These 1-inch thick boards are milled round on the front side instead of being square, and are usually 11 inches wide. The carpenter will precisely cut each tread for a tight fit. The treads are nailed onto the precut stair rise incline. The standard incline per step is 7 inches. The old 7-11 rule for building a stairway is 7 inches up and 11 inches wide.

If you are planning to have carpet on your stairs with either side of the treads stained, there are precut sections of oak tread available that can be installed on the ends which will save you money, when compared to buying solid oak treads which are rather expensive.

The next area of work to be performed on the staircase is fitting and fastening the posts. The posts are called newels. Newels are made from several types of wood and are milled into many different styles. Each newel base is precisely cut and fitted into its place in the layout. The carpenter should use at least one-fourth inch lag bolts to fasten the newels to the floor and staircase frame. A staircase should be tight and sturdy and should not wobble.

Once the newels are secured in place, holes are then measured and drilled into the ends of the stairtreads, the bottom side of the banister and the finish board on the floor that is called nosing.

Pickets are also called balusters and, like newels, are available in several wood types and styles. Prices can range from about $3.50 each for a plain simple picket to approximately $18 each for ornate, lathed balusters with square bases. That can really add up when you figure that balusters should be on 5-inch centers.

To add elegance to the bottom of your staircase, especially if it is in the foyer of your house, you can have either side or both sides of the bottom of the staircase designed to roll out. This is accomplished by having an extra wide bottom step that is rounded on the end or ends, and covered from the tread to the floor, usually in oak veneer. This roll out base step has enough room on the end or both ends, if it is a double, to accommodate as many as seven pickets. The carpenter will drill holes into the base step to mount and fasten the pickets. The pickets will be placed so that they form a semicircle as they roll to the outside of the staircase. The top of the pickets will be fitted into a special cut and prefabricated curve piece called a valute. The valute looks like the letter J and should be the same mill style as the baluster or pickets that it is fastened to.

This staircase jargon may be confusing as you are reading, but once you begin looking in catalogs to select from the many different styles, it will make more sense to you. A beautiful staircase will add a lot to the look of your house once it's finished.

To help you become familar with the basic staircase parts, we have included an illustration on the following page.

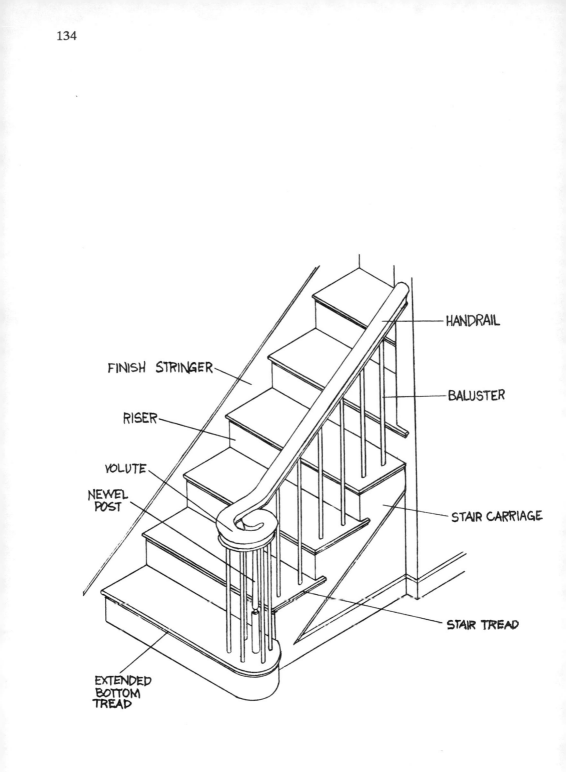

HANDRAIL

FINISH STRINGER

BALUSTER

RISER

VOLUTE

NEWEL
POST

STAIR CARRIAGE

STAIR TREAD

EXTENDED
BOTTOM
TREAD

Staircase

SECTION THREE

Sweat Equity

Sweat equity is the actual work that the owner performs on an existing house or other project in the form of remodeling, or that is performed during the process of new construction. The sweat is the work you put into your project which enables you to realize the equity later when you sell. The big plus in the sweat you put out is that it saves you from shelling out money up front to the subcontractors if you were hiring them to do the work instead of you doing the work.

I have included all of the interior cosmetics plus a chapter on landscaping in this section. You may have experience in some or all of these areas and by actually doing the work yourself you will be able to save many additional thousands of dollars and experience the satisfaction of enjoying the fruit of your own labor. There were many weekends and week nights of staining, painting, wallpaper hanging, floor finishing, and landscaping, but now we look back and realize that it was all worth it.

Chapter 21

Hardwood Floor Finishing

Hardwood floor finishing requires a lot of sanding which is tedious. I had sanded only one floor before I did ours. I knew that it would be difficult and very time consuming. I also knew that I could save at least $1,000 by doing it myself. The secret to having a good finish job is to get the feel of the large floor sanding machine before you begin actually sanding on your expensive hardwood floors.

You start your floor finishing project by calling around to the equipment rental stores in your area and getting prices on the two machines that you will need. The machine that is used to sand the large areas of hardwood floors is called the heavy duty, belt floor sander. The other machine, called a floor trim, or orbit edger, is used to sand around the perimeter of the floors, next to the walls. These machines are both very expensive, which is one reason why the floor finishing is expensive to hire out. These machines together should rent for about $60 per day. One day's rental should be enough to finish sanding your floors unless you have a lot of floor area to do.

The rental store will have different grit sandpaper belts available for the large machine and different grit disks that are round for the hand edger. You will need coarse 60 grit, a medium grade 120 grit and a fine grade 200 grit for each of the applications on the floor for both machines. The people at the rental store should give you instructions for replacing the belts, disk and the operation of the machines.

Before you begin sanding on your nice tongue and groove hardwood floors, practice getting the feel of the machines on a used piece of plywood or a couple of wide boards. What you are going to be accomplishing with the sanders is leveling all of the floor slats. It's especially important to get the feel of the large floor sander. Every aspect must be performed consistently. Consistent slow walking speed and consistent pressure on the handles, allows the machine to sand the uneven slats down uniformly. If you stop, you must push the handles down to raise the sanding drum or else it will continue sanding in that spot and create a 9-inch wide pit in your floor. Whenever you begin sanding, allow the machine to gradually make contact with the floor until you feel the sander is at the right pressure. I saved a lot of time by learning to pull the sander backwards. Whenever I would reach the end of the room, I would raise the sanding drum and simply roll the machine over nine inches to the next pass, instead of having to turn all the way around and line to begin another pass. By doing it that way, it allows a person to use different sets of muscles in the legs and back, which also helps make the job less strenuous.

After you have thoroughly sanded the floor with the heavy floor machine using the coarse sandpaper, take the edging sander and go around the edges of the walls using the coarse sandpaper disk. There is not any special trick to using this orbit sander other than you don't want to apply too much pressure, which will cause pitting. After you have completely sanded all of the edges, you can begin again with the heavy drum sander using the medium grit sandpaper belts. Follow this procedure until you have completely finished with the edger using the final fine sandpaper disk. I found that when I took breaks, I could tell how much more sanding I needed to do by rubbing my hands across the slats. I'm no perfectionist, so I have some places that aren't perfectly smooth. One thing I made sure my wife and I both understood, was that it is impossible to build a perfect house.

I recommend that if you have hardwood floors in your kitchen, schedule your machine sanding work before the cabinet makers install the base cabinet units. It makes the sanding job a lot less time consuming and I feel you get a better job.

The way I protected the machine sanded floor from stain, paint and whatever else was on people's feet as they were coming in and out of the house, was to tape sections of thick mill neoprene plastic down to the floor. This works really good. When I was ready to begin applying polyurethane floor finish to the hardwood floors that I had sanded, I took a utility knife and cut the plastic along the edges of the cabinet bases and the base molding, to reveal a sanded floor ready for floor finish.

Once you have sanded your floor to your satisfaction, the floor finish can be applied. I finished our hardwood floors late in the project, just prior to having the kitchen appliances brought in. Before you begin to apply the finish you have chosen, vacuum the floors thoroughly and then damp mop the floors and allow time for drying.

There are several oils and sealers that can be put on hardwood floors for a final finish. The oils require waxing and give a higher gloss shine than the sealers such as polyurethane. I'm not particularly partial to high gloss anything, so I chose the low maintenance route using clear polyurethane. All that it requires is damp mopping.

I selected a semi-gloss, hard finish polyurethane called Fabulon®. Debbie and I decided that the floors were too light in color, so I mixed a little of the stain we used on our kitchen cabinets into the polyurethane, which gave it a tint. I put on my knee pads and began painting the sealer on the floors using a 4-inch wide china bristle brush. We were excited at how well the darker slats in the floors blended with our stained cabinets. I allowed the floors to dry for two days and returned with a sheetrock wall sander. This handy tool has a handle with a pad attached on the end that a piece of sandpaper can be clamped to. Using fine sandpaper, I quickly went over the floor, sanding down air bubbles, dust particles and dirt. We repeated the whole process of vacuuming and wet mopping and then brushing on a second coat of polyurethane. On the second application, I used a lot less stain tint to get the finished look that we wanted. The whole process was repeated again after two days of drying. The third application of polyurethane was the final coat on our beautifully finished hardwood floors in the kitchen and foyer.

It's hard work but worth it to me. When I look at those finished floors, I remember the drops of sweat that would splatter onto the polyurethane and be blended in with the brush strokes. I also remember how important it was to save that $1,000!

Chapter 22

Staining Cabinetry and Trim Moldings

I didn't know anything about **staining** wood until we began our construction project. I sought help from a man in our area who has long had the reputation of being the best stain man around. With his 27 years of experience working with all types of decors and personalities, he knows what it takes to produce the look people want in stained wood. I will share with you the experience that he shared with me and also a truly beautiful stain formula for white oak and white pine.

I highly recommend that you stain or paint all of your trim moldings before it is sawed and nailed up by the trim carpenters. If you are painting the walls of your house yourself, it simply makes the overall job much easier.

I hired our stainmaster to give me instructions at first. Later I decided to offer him the job of staining and finishing our kitchen cabinets and mantle. They are constructed of solid white oak boards and white oak plywood. The cost of the cabinets was enough that I didn't want to risk ruining them with my inexperience. I felt more comfortable staining the doors, trim moldings, staircase and downstairs vanity. My father-in-law helped me by staining the first floor windows.

Our stainmaster taught me how to prepare soft wood for staining. Soft woods, such as white pine, bass wood or fir are used for base, chair-rail and crown trim moldings. Since these woods are softer and more porous than harder woods like oak, they will absorb stain a lot easier and faster. When the soft wood lumber is milled into the different moldings, the heart wood of the tree which is much harder, is milled along with the softer layers. If soft wood moldings aren't treated with a process called wash coating before staining, the softer layers of the molding will stain a lot darker than the harder areas. This is called "splotching" and does not look good.

I began preparing the moldings to be stained by sanding and inspecting each piece for cracks. The wash coat solution is a mixture of nine parts mineral spirits to one part polyurethane. A 6-ounce measuring cup works good when using a new unused gallon paint can for measuring the wash coat solution. I applied one generous application of the wash coat mixture to all the white pine trim, the doors and the birch plywood vanity. This sealed the wood so that the stain, when applied, would be absorbed uniformly throughout the piece of wood. The wash coat was not necessary on the mantle or kitchen cabinets due to the hardness of the white oak.

The stainmaster and I experimented for a few hours mixing and testing **stains** in order to create two stain formulas that would match the two different types of wood we were staining. We wanted all the stained wood in our house to be a uniform, warm, rich brown color. Warm, rich brown may not be the color stain for you, but in order to obtain the color you want, you really have to do some testing on the types of wood you are planning to stain.

Once we had the right formulas for our taste in wood types, I began staining the wash coated trim moldings. I brushed the stain onto one piece of trim at a time using a china bristle brush. By the time I would go from one end of a 16-foot piece of trim to the other, it was time to wipe it with a soft cotton wiping cloth. I would then place the stained piece on saw horses to dry.

About every 10 minutes, while you are staining, it is important to stir the stain. If you don't, the heavy pigmentation in the stain will settle to the bottom, and as the stain in the can is used up, it will become darker and darker.

Our stainmaster began his work by thoroughly sanding the already sanded cabinets and mantle. He said cabinetry wood should be as smooth as furniture. After his sanding, we vacuumed the cabinets thoroughly. He stained the cabinets and mantle using the special formula that we created. The formula that I will share with you toward the end of this chapter brought out the grain in the white oak wood beautifully. After the stain dried, he did a light sanding before he applied a coat of sanding sealer.

Sanding sealer is important to put on over stained wood because it does exactly as its name implies. It seals the stain to the wood so you can sand with fine sandpaper to create a smooth finish. After the sanding sealer is applied, wood putty should be mixed and put in over the holes where the finish nails have been set. Our stainmaster showed me how to mix the different colors of wood putty in order to find the right combination that matched the stained wood.

The wood putty is an important cosmetic that is used to fill in the joint cracks and small holes where the finish nails have been set. The finish carpenters should set all of the finish nails in the wood approximately one-eighth inch below the surface of the wood. The wood putty color should be as close to the stain color as possible, so that once the wood is finished, it's difficult to detect where the holes have been.

After applying the wood putty to the cracks and nail set holes, he did another light sanding on the cabinets and mantle. It was now time to apply a coat of clear polyurethane. The polyurethane provides hardness and another layer of sealant. He went over the cabinets and mantle a final time sanding with steel wool rather than fine paper. He applied the second and last coat of polyurethane which gives the wood a finish that is furniture quality. I chose low luster polyurethane because it adds depth to the wood grain without being high gloss shiny.

The finishing procedure that was performed on the cabinets and mantle was performed on all of the other stained trims and staircase in the house. We are very pleased with the stained wood in our house. It was a great learning experience for me and by doing most of the work myself, we saved another $2,000.

The formulas for **staining** white oak and white pine begin with a fruitwood stain base. The formula will have to be mixed at a Pittsburgh Paint® store. The formula is size 01, which is for one gallon. For experimentation, ask the salesperson to mix a one-half pint can for you to try on your wood. The line code is No. 77302, which is the Pittsburgh Paint's formula for semi-gloss fruitwood stain. The color tints are L-4, which is 4 drops of L brown; D-10, which is 10 drops of D green; and W-10, which is 10 drops of W white. This stain in the can looks like chocolate milk. It is the very best stain formula for white oak that I have ever seen.

To make the stain we used on white pine trim, we mixed one-half part of the fruitwood formula that we used for the white oak, to one-half part of Minwax® dark walnut. This stain formula blended almost identically to the fruitwood formula that we used on the white oak cabinets and mantle. In our kitchen, at the top of the oak cabinets, is white pine crown molding. The two different stains on these two different woods are so closely matched, that people think it's all the same wood and stain.

The best way to accomplish the stained wood look you want is to experiment. I prepared scrap pieces of molding by sanding and wash coating them. Then I would mix teaspoons of different stains together in baby food jars. By trying many combinations I began getting closer to what I liked and thought would be right for our house. The size of the rooms are significant in deciding the shade of stain to use. The darker stains are more appealing when used in larger rooms, lighter stains in smaller rooms.

Be creative. Staining wood is a type of art form and a challenge. You also save money by doing it yourself. Remember, be sure to wash coat any soft wood before staining for a professional, uniform stain job.

Chapter 23

Interior Painting

As soon as the drywall ceilings were sprayed and the wall panels finished, we began **painting**. I wanted to have all the walls and moldings painted before the trim carpenters began. The interior painting goes much easier and quicker if you can do it before the trim is cut and nailed up. Can you imagine rolling paint on a wall with stain base, chair rail and crown moldings? We hustled and it paid off in timesavings.

The way to prepare a wall to be painted is to rub your hands over the drywall finish joints and fastener finish, to check the surface of the sheetrock. If you find places that the drywall finishers missed, take a stick sander and lightly sand these areas with fine sandpaper. This process shouldn't take long, since you are only spot sanding. Once you are satisfied the walls are smooth, vacuum the walls thoroughly with a 9-inch brush attachment on the end of the vacuum cleaner hose. This removes the accumulated dust from sanding.

I wanted to paint a lot of walls fast, so I bought a paint stick from Sears. This tool works great as long as it is thoroughly cleaned after each use. It has a medium nap roller, which is ideal for painting interior walls, and it has small holes in the roller to allow the paint to ooze out as pressure is being applied to the plunger handle. The plastic reservoir handle holds about a quart of paint that is drawn into the handle using an adapter lid that fits over a gallon of paint. Reloading is like filling a large syringe. I became so proficient with the paint stick, that I was able to roll a 12-foot by 13-foot room in about 18 minutes.

Whether you use a paint stick, sprayer or regular paint roller, the end result objective is a professionally finished wall. Make sure your coverage is even and that you roll out runs. On new walls, I recommend two coats of paint for good coverage and true color.

I had some really good help with the trim painting. My wife, her wonderful parents, my brother-in-law and a couple of friends helped. We put the first coat of paint on the finger joint moldings before the trim carpenters started to work. The second coats were applied after the trim was up and nail holes and cracks were puttied. My helpers also did a great job putting two coats of semi-gloss paint on the trim of the windows, second floor doors, vanities and closets. The hard work that our family and friends did to help us with our housebuilding project will always be cherished memories for my wife and I.

I recommend a fine china bristle brush for trim work. The professionals can use a 4-inch brush for trimming windows. I prefer a 1½ inch brush. I found that using a small can (like the size that vegetables come in) works great when **painting** trim. Apply trim paint generously to fill in the little holes and cracks. Brush out runs for a professional finish.

Doing the interior painting yourself is a lot of hard work. Our family members and friends were happy that we were able to build our dream house and were glad to give their time to help us save. By not having to hire a paint company to paint the inside of our house, we saved another $2,200.

Chapter 24

Wallpaper Hanging

Hanging **wallpaper** in a kitchen or bathroom is the icing on a cake. It makes a room look complete.

Debbie and I had hung wallpaper in some of the older houses we had rented previously. It's not really difficult to do. It is tedious making the exact cuts and requires patience to line the sheets up so the patterns match. If you don't have any experience hanging wallpaper, and don't have an experienced friend or relative to help you, there are wallpaper hanging classes that are available. These classes aren't expensive to take and give you hands-on instruction.

The standard size for wallpaper on the roll is 21 inches wide. It is available in preglued and nonglued types. I recommend the preglued.

Something that I discovered about wallpaper is that there are certainly enough patterns and designs for everyone to choose from. I just gave up and told Debbie the wallpaper decisions were all hers.

The best way to hang wallpaper is to start by buying a wallpaper hanging kit. The kit will have all the tools you will need to make the job go smoothly. Each kit should include a paper wetting tray, paper cutting knife with extra blades, a leveling brush, a sponge, a straight edge and a small roller with handle for rolling out the paper joints. Another tool that we found to be handy is a 6-inch wide putty knife.

Before you begin measuring and cutting paper, prepare the walls the same as you would for painting. I highly recommend that after you vacuum the walls, you paint them with a coat of wall sizing. This product comes in powder form, mixes with water and is sold at wallpaper stores. It allows the wallpaper to thoroughly adhere to the wall surface, and in the event that you would like to remove the paper at a later time, allows you to pull it off the wall without having to scrape the walls. It also makes the wall slick, which aids in placing the paper in the right place.

One person can hang wallpaper, but it really is easier with two or three. We were fortunate to have relatives and friends who helped out.

The best place to hang the first sheet is in an inverted corner. Measure the distance from the crown molding or ceiling to the chair rail or counter-top. Roll the paper out and add about six inches to the measurement. Reroll the paper loosely and place it in the wetting tray that is half filled with water. Separate the paper to ensure that it is thoroughly wet. Place the top of the paper in the corner and up to the ceiling or molding. Smooth the wrinkles and air bubbles out with the wide brush. Place the straight edge or wide putty knife against the wall and firm against the countertop or chair rail. Using the knife, trim off the excess paper. Wipe the paper down as needed with a slightly wet sponge.

The first sheet is usually the easiest because you aren't having to match the patterns. Be sure to buy extra **wallpaper** to allow for the waste that is discarded when matching the pattern. The amount of extra paper needed for a project can be as much as one-third, depending upon the pattern. Before you do any measuring for the second sheet, roll out your paper, place it beside the first sheet and match the pattern. Then mark the paper where it is to be cut, allowing plenty of overhang. After determining the overall length of your second sheet, you should be able to continue on with cutting and hanging paper for the remainder of the room. There will be some places, such as around molding, that will require a little more time for cutting and fitting. Take heart, you can do it!

I'll share with you a few tips we learned from our wallpaper hanging experience. Use knife blades that are really sharp. It's good to either replace or sharpen them after six or seven cuts. A dull blade can badly tear a sheet.

We used wallpaper glue along the edges even though we were using the preglued type of paper. This prevents the corners from pealing back, especially in the bathrooms where the humidity is high.

When placing the paper on the wall, be careful not to stretch it out tightly. If it is stretched out a lot when wet, it will contract as it dries and will leave cracks at the joints and edges.

Hanging the wallpaper in our house was fun. It was the final wall finish work to be completed, which meant that as soon as the carpet was installed we could move into our new dream house. We saved approximately $700 by hanging our wallpaper ourselves. It all adds up.

Chapter 25

Landscaping

I had a small **landscaping** business for 18 months during the years 1977 and 1978. I had borrowed enough money from a local bank to buy a used dump truck, tractor, trailer, box blade, disk harrow, smoothing rake and an assortment of hand tools. Having grown up on a farm, I had a lot of experience operating different types and sizes of tractors. What I've learned about landscape layout, shrubs and tree types, grading and how to create a fully landscaped yard follows.

Generally, you should be able to save from $700 to $1200 on your landscaping if you do all of the work yourself. The amount of savings will depend on how involved your project is. I recommend that you get at least three detailed, line-itemed quotes from local landscape contractors prior to the completion of your house construction. Their estimates should include the following items:

- A soil test to determine the pH of the soil, which will indicate the amount of lime and fertilizer needed for the type of grass you choose to plant.
- The number of loads of topsoil they recommend to properly build up and grade your yard.
- The amount of lime, fertilizer, and grass seed needed to prepare and sew your yard.
- The quantity, size and types of all the shrubs and trees you have decided on for the front of your house and any islands you may have in your landscape design.
- The amount of black plastic to be put around shrubs and islands to prevent grass growth.
- The amount of pine straw, pine bark or rock to be put around shrubs as a border.
- Landscape timbers, if any are to be used, for a border.
- The amount of wheatstraw, if any, which is used to help prevent erosion of freshly sewn areas that are on an incline.

- The total contract price for creating your new landscaped yard.

If you intend to do the **landscaping** yourself, it is important to have prices from landscape contractors for comparison. Everything that they specify in the quotation will be most likely what you will need if you do the job yourself. Once you have a list of all the things that you need in the quantities that you need, you can bid out your materials, such as shrubs and trees and grass seeds, among the local suppliers to get the best possible price. If you intend to do the grading yourself, and have the experience to operate a tractor, then you will want to check around for the best price for the rental of a tractor, box blade, and possibly disk harrow.

The first step to take in preparing for the landscaping of your yard, if you plan to do it yourself, is to use the elevations drawings from your house plans to work up a landscape layout. If you are not familiar with varieties of shrubs and trees, ride through subdivisions and make notes of the varieties you see in yards that appeal to you. You may even want to take pictures of yards you like or collect pictures of beautiful yards in magazines. When you visit a nursery, the attendant should be very helpful in identifying the varieties you like. He or she will also be helpful in making suggestions to you as to what varieties go well together, and the types that should be planted in shaded or non-shaded areas.

The format for drawing a landscape layout really doesn't differ from one style house to another. I would use the same format for a contemporary as for a traditional house, but would substitute different varieties. I would begin the layout by working on the corners of the house. The corners, and sometimes either side of the steps, should have taller varieties of shrubs. The taller varieties are spiny Greek Juniper, Savannah holly, Cleyera Japonica, Camellia, Grecians, Hollywood juniper, Gardenia, arborvitae and American holly.

I would then begin drawing in shorter growing varieties that would be planted under windows and in the background area near the foundation of the house. Varieties that can be used in these areas are azaleas, boxwoods, compactas, andora juniper, helleri, varigated boxwood, acuba, and pittosporum.

To finish the layout, small dwarf varieties of shrubs and border plants are selected to be placed in between and in the foreground of the larger shrubs, and along sidewalks. The varieties I recommend for these areas are dwarf azaleas, yaupon holly, dwarf helleri, liriope, blue rug juniper, periwinkle, and all the many varieties of bulb flowers, such as tulips, lilies, and jonquils.

There are many other species and varieties of shrubs and flowers that are available for beautifying the front of your house and creating islands throughout your yard. The ones I have recommended are some of the most popular, especially in the sunbelt areas.

There are many varieties of ornamental **landscape** trees available that you can plant to help balance your yard and to create islands. The varieties I like for these purposes are dogwoods, Japanese maples, Bradford pears, crabapples, plums, river birches, Canadian hemlocks, sugar maples, tulip poplars, and white pine.

Varieties of shrubs and trees that are good to use as privacy borders are red tip and green augustrums, wax myrtles, Leyland cypress, wood myrtles, arborvitae, red cedars, pines, poplars, and large species of boxwoods, arborvitae, and azaleas.

If you have decided to hire a landscape contractor to grade, prepare and seed your yard, you will not save as much money, but you will not have to do as much hard work either. Some of the hardest work I've ever done was landscaping yards for general contractors and new homeowners. If you have decided to do the entire landscaping project yourself, and haven't ever landscaped a yard before, I have listed for you the step-by-step procedures a little later in this chapter.

I want to emphasize the importance of being extremely careful while operating a tractor. One slip while operating a tractor near a house could cause a lot of damage and possible injury.

The going rate for the rental of a small tractor, blade, harrow (if needed), root rake (if needed), and lime/fertilizer spreader, is approximately $150 total per day. A day generally is figured at 10 hours. I found the ideal size tractor for landscaping to be a Ford 3000 or Massey Ferguson 135. These tractors work well in tight places and have enough power to pull and grade dirt with a box blade.

Before you bring equipment onto your yard to begin grading, the yard should be clean of trash and debris. If your yard is wooded, and you are only grading a small area around your house, remove as many roots and limbs as feasible. You will definitely need to put flagged stakes up to mark the location of the **septic tank**, if you have one, and the water meter box. Look over your yard and plan the best route for the truck driver delivering topsoil to use in order to dump the dirt in the most needed areas.

The following is a step-by-step procedure for grading, preparing, and seeding the soil and for tree and shrub planting.

- Thoroughly disc the yard to loosen the soil.
- Have the purchased topsoil brought in; a light sandy loam soil works

better and will drain better than a dark, heavy soil.

- Have the truck driver who is delivering the dirt pull off as the truck is dumping so the pile won't be so high.
- Begin back-filling and grading by pulling the new topsoil with the box blade up to the sides of the foundation all the way around the house.
- Back the tractor up perpendicular to the foundation and then drop the box blade in front of the piles and push the dirt up to the foundation.
- Raise the blade; back up to within a foot of the side of the house and lower the blade.
- Slowly pull the dirt away from the house by skimming and making long pulls out to the yard perimeters; this should create a higher grade at the foundation, and gently sloping to the property lines.
- Tilt the blade by adjusting the turn crank on the right-hand three-point hitch arm of the tractor; grade the swells on the property lines to provide drainage.
- Apply the predetermined amount of fertilizer and lime with either a hand-spreader sower, or if you have a large area, you will need a three-point hitch spreader.
- After the lime and fertilizer is spread on the ground, lightly disk it in with the disk harrow, which will mix the fertilizer, lime and soil together.
- At this point, go to the perimeters of the yard or the area that you are working and have graded, and get down on your knees and look back to the house to see if the yard has good grade and if there are any low spots that need filling.
- Hook up the box blade again and lightly pull dirt around the whole yard to smooth it out; you may choose to use the root rake implement for this final smoothing.
- Sow your predetermined grass seed with a hand-cranked spreader or sower, except in the areas where you plan to plant shrubs and to make islands.
- Begin hand raking your yard with a root or rock rake at the foundations and rake back to the outside perimeter of the yard; this will lightly cover the grass seeds to enable better germination.
- Unless the area that you are seeding is very large, you should be able to finish this part of the **landscaping** in one day with a helper, that way, you can return the equipment and be charged for just one day's use.
- After your shrubs are delivered to your yard, place them in their proper places by referring to your shrub and tree layout.
- Back off about 100 feet and adjust the plants to your liking.
- Allow at least three feet from the foundation wall to the center of the

shrubs for growth.

- Dig the holes for the shrubs at least a third larger than the root ball on the shrubs; make sure the soil in the bottom of the holes is loose. Fill the holes about one-half full with water.
- Remove the plastic containers and place the plants in the holes, arranging them with the prettiest sides facing away from the house.
- Fill in dirt around the shrubs, and with your feet, pack it down so that it is firm.
- Smooth the dirt around the schrub beds with your root rake.
- Roll out black plastic beside the row of shrubs.
- Take a knife and make slits in the plastic and work the plastic around the shrubs, bringing the plastic up to the edge of the foundation; the amount of plastic that you will need for the foreground will be determined by how large a bed you choose to make.
- Shovel some dirt around the perimeter of the plastic to help keep it in place.
- If you are using **landscape** timbers, put them down along the perimeters of the bed.
- Put down at least four inches of pine straw, or two inches of pine bark or rocks for the bed cover.
- Be sure everything you have planted is watered every three days, depending upon the climate conditions and the type of grass you have selected.

Bermuda grass will need to be kept wet for about 30 days. Centipede grass should be kept wet for about 60 days. If you live in a climate that has four seasons, and you are landscaping in the winter, plant rye grass as a cover to help prevent erosion. It's better to wait until spring to plant permanent lawn grasses. The minimum temperature at night should be approximately 65 degrees if you are planning to plant bermuda or centipede.

It takes about two years to develop a good stand of grass, whatever variety you use. Most likely, there will be some settling in your yard, whether you hire a professional or if you do it yourself. It is a good idea to reserve a part of a truck load of topsoil to have on hand for touching up settled areas.

Enjoy your yard as it beautifully grows. It's a lot of hard work when you create your yard yourself. You will receive great satisfaction and enjoyment by realizing the fruit of your labor from the contracting and any other work you do yourself that helps develop your dream place.

Conclusion

Thanks again for buying this book of information and instruction. **Understanding Home Construction** was written to educate you, the person considering self-contracting your house building project. It's very important that you have a thorough understanding of everything associated with self-contracting and general knowledge of residential building. Comprehending the whole process is necessary so that you can make a rational, sound decision to either pursue the challenge of self-contracting or hire a licensed contractor.

I hope that you have been able to understand from this book that starting your project begins with months of detailed planning and research. This is necessary so that you will be prepared when the actual work begins. A person committed to self-contracting needs to be totally confident that the pre-construction homework has been done and he/she has the knowledge to resolve any problems that may develop.

What you will gain by contracting your project is the saving of a substantial amount of money or the option to build more house for the same amount of money you had allotted. Also you will have accomplished a major task in your life with the satisfaction of knowing you were the main person responsible for making a dream come true.

I conclude with these final words of inspiration. Believe in your Maker and yourself. Don't let anyone or anything steal your dreams. For dreams are the creative inner expressions from which great things are often accomplished.

Take care and best wishes to you as you pursue the building of your home.

Glossary

Acre—measure of land which is 4,840 square yards or 43,560 square feet or having four sides which average 208.7 feet each.

Adjustable Rate Mortgage—also known as a variable rate mortgage which is a loan involving a payment plan that allows the lender to periodically adjust the interest rate in accordance with certain factors which normally reflect trends in general market interest rates.

Airway—a space between roof insulation and roof boards for movement of air.

Anchor Bolts—bolts to secure a wooden seal plate to concrete or a masonry floor or a wall.

Appraised Value—an estimate of the value of property, such as a house.

Apron—the flat member of the inside trim of a window placed against the wall immediately beneath the stool.

Attic Ventilators—in houses, screened openings provided to ventilate an attic space. They are located in the soffit area as inlet ventilators and in the gable ends or along the ridge as outlet ventilators. They can also consist of power-driven fans used as an exhaust system.

Back-fill—the replacement of excavated earth into a trench around and against a foundation.

Baffle—an air space between the roof sheathing and the roof insulation in an attic.

Balusters—usually small, vertical pickets in a railing used between a top rail and the stair treads or a bottom rail.

Base or Base Molding—a wide molding placed against the wall around a room next to the floor to finish properly between the floor and the wall.

Base Shoe—a molding used next to the floor on interior baseboard molding, sometimes called a carpet strip.

Batten—narrow strip of wood used to cover a joint in interior and exterior vertical siding.

Batter Boards—sticks and cords used as guides by masons in making footings and foundations.

Boxing—the finish work of framing carpenters which involves nailing fascia boards and riped 1/4" plywood to close-in the eaves and gable ends of the roof of a house. Soffit vents are installed in this process.

Breaker—an electrical circuit breaker which is installed in a panel box that performs the same service as a fuse.

Brick Veneer—the exterior finish of a structure that is made of brick instead of wood, vinyl or masonite siding.

Bridge Loan—a short-term loan to bridge the time between the purchase of one house and the sale of another.

Bridging—the "X" shaped double pieces of wood or steel which brace joists to prevent lateral movement.

Building Code—regulations established by local governments setting fourth the structural requirements for buildings.

Building Line—a line fixed at a certain distance from the front and/or sides of a lot, beyond which no building can project.

Building Paper—black, permeable felt paper which is water repellent, but not waterproof; used between finish flooring and sub-flooring and between roofing plywood and shingles.

Casing—molding of various widths and thicknesses used to trim door and window openings at the jams.

Certificate of Title—an attorney's report or account of title based upon his examination of applicable public records. In it the attorney reports that record title to certain real property has been examined and that marketable fee simple title does or does not exist. The certificate also contains standard and special exceptions relating to matters effecting the title.

Checking—fissures or cracks that may appear with age in many exterior paint coatings; at first superficial, but in time may penetrate entirely through the coating.

Chip Board—a building material made of wood chips and plastic available in 4 x 8 feet sheets and in thicknesses from 3/8 inch to 3/4 inch or more.

Clear Title—a title of any property, such as land or a house, that is free of liens, mortgages, judgments or any other encumbrance.

Closing—the consummation or completion of a transaction involving the sale or exchange of real estate; may be accomplished either at a closing meeting attended by the various parties or agents, or by way of an escrow closing. At closing, title to the property is formally transferred to the purchaser and all financial matters relevant to the transaction are settled.

Collateral—something of value which is pledged or provided as security for a contractual obligation to grantee performance; the real estate which is mortgaged to secure the repayment of a debt evidenced by a promissory note.

Color Run—materials produced using the same batch of dye, such as bricks, carpet, or paint.

Compaction Test—a test of soil samples taken from where a footing is to be poured to check for stability of a future foundation.

Contract Price—a pre-agreed set price for a service or a product.

Corner Braces—diagonal braces at the corners of framed structures to stiffen and strengthen the wall.

Course—a row of bricks.

Crawl Space—a narrow rectangular access space under a house, porch, or in an attic.

Crown Molding—a decorative trim molding installed at the top of a wall up against the ceiling.

Dentil Molding—a type of crown molding.

Dormer—outer section of attic room that projects through the slant of the roof which is suitable for windows or other openings.

Double Glazing—windows with double panes of glass with sealed edges so no air can penetrate between the windows.

Double-hung Windows—type of windows with two sashes which slide vertically and are counterbalanced by springs.

Draw—a percentage of a term loan (usually a construction loan) paid by a lender for a portion of work or services completed.

Drip Cap—a molding placed on the exterior top side of a door or window frame to cause water to drip beyond the outside of the frame.

Dry-in—a stage in residential construction at which time the building has a roof and is protected from the elements.

Drywall—also called sheetrock, gypsum board, a wall board. It is made from gypsum plaster with a special paper on both sides, available in the dimensions of 4 x 8 feet, 4 x 10 feet, and 4 x 12 feet, and comes in different thicknesses of generally 1/2 inch and 5/8 inch. Drywall or sheetrock is nailed or screwed to studs to form flat, smooth wall surfaces.

Ducts—in a house, ducts are usually round or rectangular metal pipes used for distributing warm or cool air from the heating and cooling systems. Ducts are insulated for energy efficiency.

Earnest Money—a sum paid by the prospective purchaser of real estate as evidence of good faith; usually paid to the broker or seller at the time an offer is made.

Easement—a right to use the lands owned by another person for a special purpose, such as a right of way to go across the property of anther or a city utility line.

Eaves—the margin or lower part of a roof projecting over the exterior wall.

Equity—the difference between what you owe on something and what it is actually worth.

Expansion Joint—a strip of material used to separate blocks or sections of concrete to prevent cracking due to expansion as a result of temperature changes.

Fascia Board—the flat vertical board at the edge of a roof that is nailed to the ends of rafters. This board is part of boxing a roof.

Fire Stop—wood block that is nailed between studs to prevent updraft in the event of fire and minimize its progress.

Flashing—sheet metal or other material used in roof and wall construction to protect a building from water seepage.

Flue—the space or passage in a chimney through which smoke, gas, or fumes ascend.

Footing—a mass of concrete below the frost line supporting the foundation or base of a house. A footing will usually have reinforced steel bars and be 16 inches wide and 8 inches deep.

Foundation—the supporting portion of a structure below the first floor construction, or below grade, including the footings.

Frame Construction—using lumber to erect the vertical walls, ceilings, roof and floors of a building.

Framing—the construction of the skeleton of a building which includes the walls, floors, ceiling and roof.

Front Footage—a property measurement for sale or evaluation purposes consisting of the number of feet on the street or road frontage.

Frost Line—the depth of frost penetration in soil. The depth varies in different parts of the country. Footings should be placed below this depth to prevent movement.

Gable—angled wall section at the end of a peaked roof.

Gable Roof—pitched roof with equal angles from the ridge board.

Gambrel Roof—a roof with two planes on each side of the ridge board, sometimes called a Dutch roof.

Girder—a large or principal beam of wood or steel used to support concentrated loads at isolated points along its length.

Glass, insulated—double panes of glass with sealed edges and evacuated air space between them.

Grade—the degree of earth surface sloped around a building.

Grout—a thin cement that fills in the spaces between tiles and other masonry parts set close together.

Gypsum Board—see Drywall.

Header—any beam or structural member at the top of an opening above windows and doors or other openings in a house or building.

Hearth—the inner or outer floor of a fireplace, usually made of brick, tile, or stone.

Heat Pump—a system for heating and cooling a building which utilizes heat strips and an air-conditioning condenser to heat or cool the air, depending on the thermostat setting. The system will usually have an air handler which will push the air throughout the air duct system that is in the building.

Joist—one of a series of parallel beams, usually two inches in thickness, used to support floor and ceiling loads, and supported by larger beams, such a girders, or bearing walls.

Joist hanger—metal hangers which support the ends of joists and keep them flushed with walls to which they are attached.

Kiln Dried Lumber—lumber dried in an oven-like building which reduces the amount of water to a desirable level. A freshly cut stud at the mill is 2 x 4 inches but is reduced to 1 $1/2$ x 3 $1/2$ inches after kiln drying and will have a moisture content of between 6% to 12%.

Lattice—a framework of thin, crossed wood or metal strips.

Load Bearing Capacity—the amount of weight a particular piece of lumber, steel, or soil can withstand without breaking or bending beyond its design.

Load Bearing Partition—an interior wall that is essential to the the support of the structure above it.

Loan Closing—the signing of legal documents with a lender in order to receive a loan, is usually in the presence of an attorney.

Manager's Contract—a contract with a general contractor by which he agrees to act as a manager to construct a house. Under such a contract, the individual building the house is able to remain the primary general contractor (also called Contractor Associate).

Masonry—stone, brick, concrete, hollow tile, concrete block or other similar building materials or combination of these materials, bonded together with mortar to form a wall, pier, buttress or similar mass.

Moisture Barrier—material used to retard the movement of water vapor into walls and to prevent condensation in them. This material is usually polyethylene.

Molding—long lengths of lumber milled at a lumber yard to be used as interior trim in a house or office building. Molding is available in many styles and types such as crown molding, chair rail, and base molding.

Mortar—a mixture of cement, sand, and water used between bricks or concrete blocks to hold them together for the purpose of making a wall, such as a foundation.

Newel Post—a post at the start or the end of a stairway that railing is attached to.

Non-bearing Wall—a wall supporting no load, other than its own weight.

Nosing—the rounded front edge of a stair tread.

Origination Fee—a one time fee charged to a borrower by a lender for making a mortgage loan, usually computed at 1% of the loan amount.

Panel—an electrical panel to which all of the wires for the different circuits of a house or building are pulled and connected with breakers, which will eliminate overload of electricity in the different wiring circuits. Also, in house construction, plywood or dry wall or sheetrock used to make flat wall surfaces are in panels.

Percolation Test—a soil test to determine if soil will absorb and drain water sufficiently for use of a septic tank.

Pier—a column of masonry, usually made of cement blocks that are rectangular, which is used to support other structure members, such as girders.

Pitch—rate of rise or slope of a roof. A rise of 6 inches per foot is called one-quarter pitch.

Plat—a map of a division of land into blocks and lots.

Plate—seal plate: a horizontal member anchored to a masonry wall; sole plate: bottom horizontal member of a framed wall; top plate: top horizontal member of a framed wall supporting ceiling joists, rafters or other members.

Plumb—exactly perpendicular; vertical.

Plywood—a piece of wood made of several layers of veneered wood joined with glue, and usually laid with the grain of adjoining pieces at right angles. Almost always, an odd number of plies are used to provide balanced construction.

Point—one percent of a mortgage loan. Also discount points, which is a fee charged by a lender, usually paid by the borrower, to increase the yield on mortgage loans which have below market interest rates.

Polyethylene—plastic film, used in home construction to provide a moisture barrier.

Polyurethane—a type of liquid preservative painted on wood or masonry work, which is used as a moisture barrier and preservative.

Purchase Contract—an offer to purchase that has been accepted by the seller and has become a binding contract between seller and buyer. Also known as a sales contract.

Quote—a prearranged guaranteed price for work to be performed or for the price of products that are to be bought.

R-value—a measure of a material to impede or resist heat flow through it.

Radiant Heating—a form of heating in which electric heating cables or copper pipes bearing hot water are buried in a concrete floor. This type of heating is generally associated with an active solar heating system.

Rebar—steel or iron rods used to give inner strength to concrete.

Rafter—one of a series of structural members of a roof designed to support roof loads. The rafters of a flat roof are sometimes called roof joists.

Raised Panel—a panel beveled on all four sides; usually seen on interior doors and on the doors of cabinets.

Recording Fee—a fee charged to record legal documents, such as deeds, that are in a place of permanent records, such as a county courthouse.

Reflective Insulation—sheet insulation material with one or both surfaces covered with comparatively low heat emissivity, such as aluminum foil. When used in building construction, the surfaces face air spaces, reducing the radiation across the air space.

Reinforcing Rod—steel rods placed in concrete footings, slabs, or beams to increase their strength.

Restrictive Convenant—a clause of limitation in a deed providing that land will be used or not be used in a certain way.

Ridge Beam—central beam at the top of a pitched roof to which all rafters are fastened.

Riser—the vertical pieces that connect the treads of steps.

Rod Chair—formed wire in the shape of a chair used to elevate steel rods that are placed in a footing trench prior to pouring concrete.

Roof Sheeting—the boards or sheet materials fastened to the roof rafters on which the shingles or other roof covering is laid. Generally, roof sheeting is exterior plywood.

Roof Truss—triangular wooden-shaped frame with integral bracing which takes the place of rafters and ceiling joists, and permits non-load bearing partitions.

Rough-in—the installation of plumbing, heat ducts, or wiring in the walls, floors or ceilings of a framed building before the walls, floors or ceilings are covered with drywall, plaster or paneling.

Sash—a single light frame part of a window containing one or more panes of glass.

Septic System—a system which disposes of sewage from a house or building utilizing a large cement tank and several underground drain lines throughout an area of ground surrounding the building.

Shake Shingles—a hand split shingle, usually of cedar wood, which has a rough surface and is split with the grain.

Sheathing—the structural covering, usually plywood, that is used over studs or rafters of a structure.

Shim—a thin wedge of wood or metal used to fill in a space, usually to make something level.

Sill—the lowest member of the frame of a structure, resting on the foundation and supporting the floor joints or the uprights of the wall; the member forming the lower side of an opening, such as a door sill or window sill.

Soffit Vent—an air vent that is in the underside of a roof overhang which allows air circulation under the roofing and between the roof rafters. This vent prevents heat build up and rotting of the wood members in the roof.

Span—the distance between structural supports such as walls, columns, piers, beams, girders, and trusses.

Square—a unit of measure; one hundred square feet; usually applies to roofing material. Shingles are generally packed to cover one hundred square feet and are sold on that basis.

Stool—a flat molding fitted over the window sill at the bottom part of a window frame that connects the interior window sill and slopes downward and outward.

Strike—hardwood on a doorjamb that receives the latch or bolt of the lock.

Stud—vertical 2-inch by 4-inch or 2-inch by 6-inch lumber that is used in wall framing and is placed on 16-inch centers. For standard 8-foot walls and ceilings a precut stud will be 93-inches long.

Subdivision—a tract of land divided into smaller parcels or lots, usually for home building purposes.

Sub-floor—boards or plywood laid on floor joists over which a finished floor is to be laid.

T and G—boards or plywood sheets that have tongues and grooves in their edges to provide a close fit.

Take-off—the figuring of a list of materials used for a particular phase of construction, such as the number of studs that will be needed for the building of a particular house.

Tax-Stamp—a stamp affixed to a legal document which indicates that a tax has been paid.

Temporary Service—the temporary electrical service used during the construction of a building. The temporary service consists of several receptacles mounted on a service pole which is then connected to the utility lines.

Termite Shield—a shield, usually of non-corrodible metal such as aluminum, placed in or on a foundation wall or other mass of masonry, or around pipes to prevent passage of termites.

Threshold—a strip of wood or metal with beveled edges used over the finished floor and the sill of exterior doors.

Title Insurance—an insurance policy that protects the owner of real estate from any loss due to defects in his title.

Toenailing—to drive a nail at a slant with the initial surface in order to permit it to penetrate into a second member.

Treads—the horizontal part or top of each step in each stairway.

Trim—the finished materials in a house or building such as moldings.

Truss—a prefabricated roof support consisting of two rafters, a cross timber and bracing all nailed together in one piece.

Underlayment—a material placed under finished coverings, such as flooring or shingles, to provide a smooth even surface for applying the finish. This term generally applies to plywood that is put on top of the sub-floor.

Vapor Barrier—see Moisture Barrier.

Vent—a pipe or duct which allows flow of air as an inlet or an outlet. Pipe vents are required for all drainage plumbing, and foundation vents are required for all types of foundations.

Volute—a curved stair-rail end that rests on the newel post. A volute will generally have several pickets also attached to it and base step of a staircase.

Wallboard—gypsum board, drywall, or sheetrock.

Waterproofing—the application of different types of materials which will make a foundation impervious to water.

Weep Holes—openings in masonry walls that permit rainwater to drain away. Weep holes are generally on four foot increments of foundation walls.

Windows:
    awning—windows hung at the top which swing outward and may or may not be operated by a rotary screw mechanism.
    casement—windows hinged on a vertical axis that swing outward.
    celestory—fixed, narrow pains usually high up on a wall.
    double hung—a sliding window in which two slashes slide up and down vertically in separate tracts.

Weather-strip—narrow sections of thin metal or other materials used to prevent infiltration of air and moisture around windows and doors.

Zoning Ordinance—a local ordinance exercising the police power of a municipal corporation or county that divides land into use classifications by zone or area and also usually regulates lot size and the placement, bulk, and height of building structures.

Index

Appraisal, 9, 43, 57
Attorney, 8, 9, 42, 55-57, 59, 68

Bank/Bankers, 41-42, 44, 45
Building Contract Form, (illus) 40
Building Permit, 61, (sample) 62

Contractor Associate, 42-45
Contracts, 37, (ex) 40
Construction Cost Budget, 33, (illus) 38-39
Construction Loan, 41-45, 56

Deed of Trust, 56
Draftsperson, 14, 84, 124
Draw, 44
Drywall, 66, 115-116

E-300 Program, 12-13, 35, 66, 82, 111, 113
Electrical/Electrician, 35, 64-65, 67, 103-107, (illus) 104
Elevations, 19, (illus) 30-31
Energy Efficient, see E-300

Floor Plan, see Plans
Footings, 34, 64, 75, (illus) 79
Foundation, 18, (illus) 24-25, 64-65, 77-78
Framing, 34-35, 65, 81-89, (illus) floor 83, wall 85, roof 87

Garage, extra room 17
Gypsum Board, see Drywall

Heating, Venting, Air Conditioning (HVAC), 13, 35, 65, 67, 97-101
House Plan, see Plans

Inspections, 57, 64-68, 75, 86, 88, 91, 106
Insulation, 66, 109-113, also see E-300
Insurance, builder's risk 45, 57; property 59; private mortgage 59; title 58

Landscaping, 36, 67, 73, 107, 149-153
Loan, 41, 42, 100; bankers 41; closing 42, 55, 68; deed of trust 56; origination fee 57-58; % of completion form (illus) 56

Materials, list 14, 19, (ex) 20-21; description form (illus) 47- 54
Moisture, barrier 65; problems 111; vapor barrier 77, 111, 113
Mortgage, 41, 55-58

Painting, 67, 145-146
Permits, 61, building (illus) 62, health department (illus) 63,103
Perspective, 18, (illus) 22-23
Plans, floor 11, 12, 18, (illus) 26-29; house 14-15, 22-32
Plaster Walls, 117
Plot Plan, 15, (illus) 16
Plumbing, 35, 64-65, 67, 93-96, rough-in (illus) 94
Porta-John, 34, 64
R-value, 109-111
Restrictive Covenant, 7-8
Roof, 12, (illus) 87, trusses 86

Septic System, 8, 34, 73, 107, 151
Sheetrock, see Drywall
Specifications, 19
Staining, 141-143
Staircase, 131-133, (illus) 134
Stud, see Framing
Subcontractor, 33-36, 61, 65-67, 77, 89, 91, 93
Survey/Surveyor, 9, 15, 34, 55, 57, 59, 68, 73

Telephone, 34
Title Search, 8, 55
Trash Container Company, 34, 64

Vapor Barrier, see Moisture

Wall Cross Section, 19, material (illus) 32, insulation (illus) 112
Wallpaper, 36, 67, 147-148
Well, 8, 13, 99

Book Order Form

Understanding Home Construction makes a great gift for anyone who is considering building a house. Additional copies are $12.00, plus $2.00 shipping & handling.

Please send _____ copy(ies) of **Understanding Home Construction.**
*N.C. residents add 6% sales tax.

❑ Personal Check
❑ Money Order
or dial 1-800-345-0096

Name _____

Address _____

City _____State_____Zip_____

Mail your order to:

Southeastern Publishing Company
2462 Stantonsburg Road
Greenville, NC 27858

Book Order Form

Understanding Home Construction makes a great gift for anyone who is considering building a house. Additional copies are $12.00, plus $2.00 shipping & handling.

Please send _____ copy(ies) of **Understanding Home Construction.**
*N.C. residents add 6% sales tax.

❑ Personal Check
❑ Money Order
or dial 1-800-345-0096

Name _____

Address _____

City _____ State_____Zip _____

Mail your order to:

Southeastern Publishing Company
2462 Stantonsburg Road
Greenville, NC 27858

Traditional Country Classic

If you like the look and floor plan design of our house in Chapter 2, and would like to order this plan to build, fill in the information below.

Check which plan you want:

❏ Garage on right   ❏ Garage on left

❏ Personal Check
❏ Money Order
❏ Visa Card No. _____
❏ MasterCard No. _____
Expiration Date: _____

Name _____

Address _____

City _____ State _____ Zip _____

The price for 6 complete sets of plans including perspective, elevations, foundation, floor plans, wall cross section and materials list is $225.00* Postage Paid.
*N.C. residents add 6% sales tax.

Mail your order to:

Southeastern Publishing Company
2462 Stantonsburg Road
Greenville, NC 27858